MULES, MINES AND
ME IN MEXICO

The sixteen and three score years 1871–1947,
the life span of the author to the
present time, have been marvelous years in which
to have lived: from horses and buggies,
tallow candles and black powder,
to push buttons and atomic bombs.
These ramblings of a mining engineer have been
plucked from memory and from
personal diaries which date back to 1886.

MORRIS B. PARKER

Morris B. Parker's

MULES, MINES AND
ME IN MEXICO

1895-1932

*Edited With an
Introduction and Notes by*
James M. Day

THE UNIVERSITY OF ARIZONA PRESS
Tucson

About the Author . . .

MORRIS B. PARKER was 24 years old when he first ventured into Mexico in 1895. Already an experienced miner and assayer, he was offered the management of an ore-buying agency in Mexico. He reminisces of the succeeding 37 years in many out-of-the-way camps of Northern Mexico. He stayed long enough to eye-witness one of Mexico's most turbulent periods of history and to make the acquaintance of leaders such as Pancho Villa, William C. Greene, and Pasqual Orozco. His memoirs of his early years in New Mexico are recorded in *White Oaks: Life in a New Mexico Gold Camp, 1880–1900.*

About the Editor . . .

JAMES M. DAY, an experienced writer and editor of history of the Southwest and Texas, joined the faculty of the Department of English, the University of Texas, El Paso, in 1967. Prior to that he was both a professor of history and Texas State Library Director of Archives. He received an M.A. in history from the University of Texas, Austin, and a Ph.D. in literature from Baylor University.

THE UNIVERSITY OF ARIZONA PRESS

Copyright © 1979
The Arizona Board of Regents
All Rights Reserved
Manufactured in the U.S.A.

Library of Congress Cataloging in Publication Data

Parker, Morris B.   1871–1957.
    Morris B. Parker's Mules, mines, and me in Mexico, 1895–1932.

    Bibliography: p.
    Includes index.
    1. Mines and mineral resources—Mexico—History.
2. Parker, Morris B., 1871–1957. 3. Mining engineers—Mexico—
Biography. I. Day, James M. II. Title. III. Title: Mules, mines,
and me in Mexico, 1895–1932.
TN28.P37 1979   338.2'092'4   [B]   79-15206
ISBN 0-8165-0626-4

To the Day Boys
George Allen, Billy Floyd, and Tommy Joe
My brothers for a lifetime

J. M. D.

Contents

MAPS

CONTENTS

Acknowledgments

Part of the fun of editing a manuscript comes from the people you meet along the way. My involvement with this manuscript has been far too lengthy, but it has been rewarding in terms of learning anew the goodness of people.

Lina Parker Mathews has exhibited some of the most persistent patience I have ever known. She has understood, where understanding was a virtue; she has urged when such was in order. She is a lady in the kindest sense of the word, and my indebtedness to her is immeasurable.

S. D. Myres, C. L. Sonnichsen, Leon C. Metz, John O. West, Lucy West, and James K. P. Mortensen all contributed to the effort by encouragement and by making money and time available for the tedious task of introducing myself to the mining industry of northern Mexico. A research grant for a semester from the University of Texas at El Paso was a boon to the cause. The librarians in the Southwest Room at the El Paso Public Library have been superb. They include Virginia Hoke, Shirley Watson, Lisa Lovelace Davis, Glennis Hinshaw, Harriet Stegner, and Mary Sarber. In the Texas State Library, the director, Dorman H. Winfrey, and the reference librarian, Ann Graves, went beyond the call of duty. Of the same stamp was Frank Schmaus of the Engineering Library, University of Texas at Austin. Those who helped with the typing are Warren Peters, Rosalinda Bernal, Otto Nieman, Phyllis Strauss, Alicia Burton, Maria Maldonado, Tony Trejo, Lori Lester, Perla Maldonado, and Kathleen O'Brien. A special note of appreciation must be voiced to the University of Arizona Press which has seen fit to carry forward this volume to publication.

Finally, to Jimmy and Joey, my sons, I express my eternal gratitude for allowing me time to take the trail in Mexico with Morris Parker, compañero.

J. M. D.

Editor's Introduction

Morris Parker's best years were spent during the time he interested himself in mining activities in northern Mexico. He was an optimistic twenty-four years of age in 1895 when his first brush with Mexico occurred; he was an established sixty-one in 1932 when he gave up on the cornucopia, when for him the magnet that was Mexico had been neutralized.

Those first two dozen years had been a magnificent training ground for the development of an engineer. Much of the story has been published in *Morris B. Parker's White Oaks: Life in a New Mexico Gold Camp, 1880–1900* edited by C. L. Sonnichsen and published by the University of Arizona Press (1971). It is a good tale and true, but there are a few additional points that can be made.

In the background are Parker's parents — Erastus Wells Parker and Emmeline Brown Parker, both of whom came from aristocratic stock. Erastus Parker, born in Danville, New York, was reared in St. Louis where the family had a successful sawmill and lumber business. He loved to travel as much as he loved fast horses, and both passions brought him some conflict when he married Emmeline Brown of Pen Yan, New York, in 1866. Her father, Morris Brown (after whom Morris Parker was named), was a prominent landowner, attorney, politician, and judge. Emmeline was a society belle, a talented pianist and singer. As a wedding present Judge Brown presented the Parkers with land that supported a substantial vineyard, expecting that the young couple would settle there. Emmeline did but Erastus would not. Instead, he divided his time between Pen Yan and St. Louis for about seven years until 1873, when he took his family to St. Louis to live. By then, the couple had three living children as follows: James H., born 1868; Frank W., born 1870; and Morris B., born 1871. They lived in St. Louis until 1882, always spending the summers at Pen Yan.

Erastus Parker did not abandon his wanderlust though, for he took a position with the United States Mail Stage Line as superintendent of the activities between Fort Worth, Texas, and San Diego, California. As such he was constantly traveling his territory, seeing to equipment and operations. It was in the midst of these activities that he happened into White Oaks, New Mexico, at a time when the gold exploration was in its infancy. Infected by this virus, he purchased the South Homestake Mine, resigned his position with the stage line, and moved his family to White Oaks.[1]

There the E. W. Parker family lived in prominence. Mrs. Parker was a talented musician, so the home naturally became a social center. Their affairs were widely reported in the newspapers of Lincoln County, and when they went to the county seat of Lincoln they had regular quarters at the Lincoln Hotel. Erastus Parker, through the years, served as a delegate to the Lincoln County Republican Convention and as a director of the White Oaks School District. In 1896 he served as Worshipful Master of White Oaks Lodge No. 20, A.F. & A.M.[2] By 1895 the troubles of mining the South Homestake were insurmountable, so shortly thereafter Erastus Wells Parker liquidated what assets he could and left White Oaks. But the White Oaks years had been good ones for the Parkers.

Morris Parker and his two brothers, James and Frank, grew to maturity there. Their mother provided them with the fundamentals of education, but Morris also studied geometry with William C. McDonald, a man destined to become New Mexico's first statehood governor and also the stepfather of Parker's wife. In 1885 the youngster went back to Pen Yan, New York, for high school. He stayed there two years before transferring to St. Louis, where he took his diploma. Major studies were languages — Greek, Latin, German, and French — and mathematics, and he developed an interest in chemistry. Between 1889 and 1892, Parker attended Colorado College at Colorado Springs, taking as much chemistry as possible, before he transferred to the Missouri School of Mines at Rollo (1892–93).[3] With formal education completed Parker returned to White Oaks in 1893, where he advertised himself as a mining engineer and practical assayer.[4] That same year, on November 29, he married Olive Genevieve McCourt.

His mature White Oaks years were interesting ones as he experimented with and applied the cyanide process of ore concentration to the working of the South Homestake Mine. Late in 1895 Parker and his two brothers went on an exploring expedition into the San Andres Mountains where they located some fine looking lead claims.[5] It was that year also that Morris and Olive Parker lost their infant daughter. When she died on September 28, they buried her in the Knights of Pythias Cemetery at White Oaks.[6] Later they had five additional children, three of whom were born in Mexico. They were named Lina, Frances, Genevieve, Margaret, and Morris, Jr.

Such was the state of life for Morris Parker when he made his first visit to Mexico in 1895, the first episode described in this reminiscence. It is significant that he entered through El Paso, for the place came to have more than perfunctory meaning for him and his family. After their stay in Nacozari, Sonora, ended in 1903, they moved to El Paso, settling first at 1213 Myrtle. Then they lived at 806 E. Rio Grande, 327 Upson Avenue, and finally 601 Upson Avenue in Sunset Heights. The last residential reference for the Parkers was in the 1909 city directory, but his offices at the Masonic Temple and the City National Bank Building are listed from 1902 to 1915. During that time Morris Parker and his brother, James, had a loose partnership in a consulting engineering firm. In 1906 Morris served a stint as president of the International Miners' Association, an organization by then holding its annual meetings in Chihuahua City but having its home office at El Paso. He wrote frequently for the *El Paso Mining Journal* even though he was often — more often than not — traveling in the Sierra Madre of Mexico. Mines which he served as consulting engineer, in addition to El Carmen and La República, included the Fortuna, North Tigre, Rosario, and Dos Cabezas. There were many others, but these were his listings in 1925 in *Who's Who in Engineering*.[7]

By the time Parker entered northern Mexico, the mining revolution of Chihuahua was well under way, though that of Sonora was just getting started. Several things were needed to bring this revolution to a peak, not the least of which were railroads. The completion of the Mexican Central Railroad in 1884 between Ciudad Juárez and Chihuahua and Mexico City provided a way to carry ore to the smelter. Then there was the Río Grande, Sierra Madre and Pacific which ran from Juárez to Casas Grandes in 1897, built by the Corralitos Land and Cattle Company. From the south came the Kansas City, Mexico and Orient building from Chihuahua to Miñaca in 1900. Finally these two roads were united in 1912 in a road that stretched from Miñaca to Temósachic to Madera to Casas Grandes. Over in Sonora, the Southern Pacific built from Nogales to Guaymas in 1882, but the line did not extend to Tepic, in Nayarit, until 1913. The only other railroads of consequence in northern Sonora were the Cananea, Yaqui River and Pacific built between Cananea and Naco with a connection near Bisbee, completed in 1901, and the road from Douglas to Nacozari, completed in 1904.[8]

These railroads were not much, but they provided substantial assistance in hauling ore from the mines and heavy equipment to the mines. All Mexican railroads at that time in Chihuahua ran essentially in a north-south direction alongside the impressive Sierra Madre, whose barrancas and peaks were not penetrated until 1961 when the Ferrocarril Chihuahua al Pacífico was finished from Chihuahua to Los Mochis. Thus, in Parker's time, there was no easy way to get from Chihuahua to Guaymas except the northern route to El Paso, then west to Nogales along the El Paso and

Southwestern and then south along the Southern Pacific. And though these lines did not penetrate the mountain fastnesses where the mines were, they still provided the essential links for the industry. It was along these roads, at Chihuahua City and Terrazas in Chihuahua and at Nacozari and Cananea in Sonora, that the smelters were located at El Paso, Douglas and Bisbee.[9] In the final analysis the smelters were the industrial mechanisms that rejuvenated and reoriented the mineral industry of Chihuahua and Sonora.

Parker's time in Mexico was truly the golden age of mining there for Americans. The policies of Porfirio Díaz which attracted foreign capital had been in effect long enough to bear fruit. Statistics prove the point. In 1868 only thirteen American-owned mining companies were in all of Mexico, a figure that bounded to 840 by 1907. American investments in Mexican mining properties in 1890 aggregated $125 million; by 1907 the figure had leaped to $800 million. Gold production alone is another indication of the growth. In 1880 Mexico produced less than one percent (0.85) of the world's gold; by 1910 it peaked at almost five percent (4.98), or 5,240,975 fine ounces. The extent of American influence can be seen in the fact that the Yankees owned three-fourths of the dividend-paying mines of the nation.

Though gold is found in both Sonora and Chihuahua, neither is a leader among the Mexican states. Chihuahua is known for its silver, lead, and zinc and while Sonora has produced its share of silver, it primarily is famous for the copper it belches forth. Chihuahua had just over one hundred mineral districts in 1911 in which were located 570 producing mines. Gold and silver bullion alone (excluding ore shipped to smelter for treatment) exceeded $800,000 per month, one-third of which was exported to the United States and England. In 1905 Chihuahua's mines produced 566,377 metric tons of ore valued at $14,765,573. It is little wonder that Chihuahua ranked first among the states of Mexico in minerals produced during the golden age. Sonora's star was later in rising, but it did shine forth. The measuring stick here is in mining claims as registered in the district offices. There were practically no mining claims in the state in 1870; by 1900 there were 1,400; by 1909 there were 5,335. Sinaloa told the same story: no claims in 1870; 415 in 1905; 1,728 in 1909.[10]

It takes no genius to discern that Parker was one of many who brought an alien culture to the Mexicans of the cities and the pueblos. Eventually it was the peasants who revolted against the policies of Porfirio Díaz and against the foreign influence those policies fostered. It was no accident that two of Parker's bullion conductors, Orozco and Villa, were among the most active of the revolutionaries, nor was it accidental that their soldiers were the miners who had labored for the foreigners and farmers who had helped feed them. The end result was Morris Parker's final lament: "Mexico was no longer for me." It was so for many Americans, after the revolution.

After 1916 his interests gradually led Parker north and westward. From 1918 to 1919 he was consulting engineer for the King and Queen Copper Company at Steins, New Mexico, and from 1919 to 1921 he served in the same capacity for California Rand Silver, Inc., at Randsburg. Thereafter, he freelanced, traveling from the West Coast of Mexico to the frozen tundra of Alaska. When he retired, home came to be Hermosa Beach, California. Mrs. Parker died there in 1955 and Morris B. Parker passed away on October 18, 1957.[11] By his own testimony, his eighty-six years had been good ones.

During his lifetime the industrial revolution contributed substantially to the quality of human life, and Morris Parker saw much of this change in the Southwest. One example is in transportation. When he first went to Mexico in 1895, Parker went alternately by stage and train; his last trip was by automobile. He witnessed the building of railroads, in fact was one of the recipients of the blessings thereof, owing to the fact that he spent so many hours in travel. Another invention that fascinated the engineer was the camera, for he always carried and used one on his travels.

It was a practical matter to Parker, for he found it easier to show a prospective investor what a mine looked like than to describe it with words. But regardless of the reason, he participated in the camera revolution, and in so doing took most of the photographs which accompany this autobiography.

The bulk of this manuscript centers on mining activity in Chihuahua and Sonora, particularly at the points where those northern Mexican states touch Arizona, New Mexico and Texas. He was personally acquainted with the political and business leaders of the region; Don Luis Terrazas and his family, Abraham González, P. Elías Calles, Pancho Villa, and Pascual Orozco, of Chihuahua; Don Venanzio Durazo of Sonora; William C. Greene, James Douglas, Jr., and Gov. George W. P. Hunt of Arizona; Gov. William C. McDonald of New Mexico; and Britton Davis of Texas. He writes of them and their humanity, but the story Morris Parker tells stresses people — working people. His humanistic approach to autobiography puts him downstage as he yields to the dramatic interaction. Colonel Greene and "Rawhide Jimmy Douglas" may be more fully portrayed in other works, but they will never have a more ardent admirer than Morris Parker. Yet, even in devotion Parker displays wit and a sharp crisp command of language to reveal the slightly humorous, sometimes ludicrous, side of mankind, playing no favorite among the ethnic groups he knew.

Morris Parker, withal, is a man well worth the study. His papers were deposited in the Huntington Library, San Marino, California, while those of his brother, James, were preserved in the Mining File of the Southwest Room of the El Paso Public Library. In the latter collection can be found many reports and letters written by Morris, whose published pieces are found mostly in the *Engineering and Mining Journal,* the *Mexican Mining Journal,* and the *El Paso Mining Journal,* which exists only in fragments now because a complete file cannot be located.

In his old age, in 1947, with his eyesight failing, Morris Parker dictated his recollections to his daughter, Lina, to whom we are indebted for their transcription and preservation and to whom Parker inscribed this tribute on the original manuscript: "To my beloved and loving daughter, Lina, without whose help and encouragement these pages would not have been written."

Lina Parker Mathews had twin sons named Morris and William. Morris became a sales representative for Hughes Aircraft in Los Angeles. When asked what he remembered about Morris Parker, his grandfather, Bill Mathews readily replied "his high principles." Quickly Bill added: "And he always smoked a pipe and had a ready wit." Somehow, for those who will come to know Morris Parker through his memoirs, those are characteristics that stand out.

JAMES M. DAY

MULES, MINES AND
ME IN MEXICO

Parker's 1895 Trip to Guanaceví

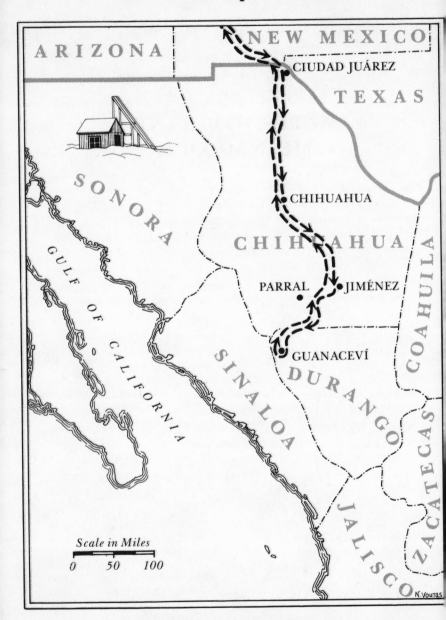

N. VOUTAS

Guanaceví, Durango, and the Barrancas of Chihuahua

MEXICO, A CORNUCOPIA IN SHAPE and substance, has been a magnet for settlers, adventurers, clerics, romantics, and tourists since history began. I was lured into that cornucopia in 1895 and from then until 1932 a goodly portion of my time was spent below the border, years before modern jazz, tinsel, and night clubs obscured the native charm, years in which that unfortunate country was emerging from its tightly woven chrysalis of subjugation through a chaotic revolutionary release to take its rightful place among the powerful nations of the world. Most of my time was spent along the trails far from civilization in out-of-the-way places among the mountain people. Regardless of progress elsewhere, they were affected little. Except for an occasional telephone line, and, in recent years, the rare sight of an airplane high in the sky, modern civilization to them was largely a matter of imported fairy tales.

My first acquaintance with one of these "out-of-the-way places" occurred when Lewis Brothers of Mexico City offered me the management of an ore-buying agency at Guanaceví[1] in the State of Durango.[2] To get there, a distance of 800 miles in all, was an enterprise in itself. From White Oaks, New Mexico, located on Baxter Mountain northeast of Carrizozo, a Concord stagecoach[3] drawn by four horses took me 90 miles to the railroad at San Antonio. Then by train,[4] a welcome change, I got to El Paso, a big and bustling town! Transportation across the Río Grande bridge to Juárez was a four-wheel streetcar drawn by two small mules.[5] The

[3]

fare was ten cents. Then, by train again, I journeyed 350 miles to Jiménez,[6] a station of the Mexican Central Railway,[7] which served as a distributing point for ranches, towns, and mining camps throughout the neighborhood. To me, however, this was the "jumping-off place" for a 210-mile stagecoach journey[8] to my destination further south, a strange land and an unknown environment.

From Jiménez the schedule called for an early start to be made long before daylight. Awakened before 3:00 A.M. by the hotel *mozo*, hardly was I dressed before a wizened old man three times my age and apparently half my strength came to carry my luggage. He was a symbol of the handy transferman found everywhere in Mexico. Waving all help aside, he hoisted my steamer trunk onto his back, put the roll of bedding and suitcase under his arm somehow, then, in a fast trot in the dark, led the way to the station, a distance of a long city block. This sight, the weight and management of any awkward load, is common in Mexico and still retains its appeal as an exhibition of effective transport.

The morning air was crisp and cold, the sort of morning that makes a cup of hot coffee enjoyable, provided one is available. Not so at Jiménez: it was to be two-and-a-half hours and 15 miles to breakfast. What we had to eat I have long since forgotten, but there I learned about Mexican coffee!

They buy their coffee *crudo* (green beans), then place it in a frying pan over an open fire in the fireplace, where the daily portion is parched. Crushed by hand between two stones, *metate* and *mano*, the ground material is boiled with as little water as possible, sometimes in a muslin bag. The boiling is continued until the mixture is almost a syrup. It is served cold from a long-spouted teapot, a tablespoon being enough. The mixture is poured into a cup which is then filled with hot water or hot milk. Like French *cafe noir* and other European coffee, Mexican coffee (*cafe negro*) is not so terrible; however, being a tenderfoot and knowing no better, I filled a *big* cup with the oily, black liquid, then added a lump of *pinoche* (crude cane sugar) and very little milk. Somehow I managed to drink the cold concentrated essence, and thereby staged a record-breaking performance in that I had no sleep for a week.

That, and the journey by coach, were both to blame. The stagecoach was a regulation Concord, having swing-roll leather springs, a high driver's seat with deep boot beneath, a trunk and baggage boot behind, iron railing around the top. It was much the same as those with which I had been familiar at White Oaks, but the balance of the makeup was different. Instead of four or six big American horses or mules, the Mexicans used their own native stock, thirteen small, mountain-bred mules. They were placed three abreast, and two were attached to the tongue of the coach, below

Parker's extended journey from Jiménez to Parral in 1895 was aboard this standard Concord stagecoach.

and in front of the driver. A new team was installed every twelve or fifteen miles. The driver held reins to the two "wheelers," a single line to each of the front, outside leaders, and flourished a long *azotilla* (black-snake whip), with which he was an accomplished master. One quick twist of his brutal whip, a snap, strike, and report like the explosion of dynamite, was a more potent factor for starting and guiding the mules than an armful of straps or reins could possibly have been.

The driver's assistant was also an expert worth watching because he was a lively kid and good runner whose main duty was to jump off and gather stones along the road. He performed this task mostly on uphill slopes where speed slowed down somewhat, and after regaining his seat alongside the driver, he would throw the stones with unfailing skill. Usually he was able to skip-jack the throw, thus hitting two or more mules with a single stone. The talents of these two, the driver and the helper, their accuracy in hitting the spot aimed at and getting results, were accomplishments worthy of acclaim by sharpshooters anywhere!

An important feature of the coach was the foot- or hand-lever brake, a cumbersome affair that was easy to operate. When in proper working order and applied, it had sufficient grip on the back wheels to produce an effect on both mules and passengers much the same as an anticipated collision or turn-over wreck. The result depended on whether his honor, the driver, wanted to stop or merely slow down!

Stations for relays, or changing mules, were 15 to 20 miles apart. Whenever fresh animals were attached to the coach, six men would hold the half-broken herd, a man with each outside mule on both sides. At the driver's sharp command to start — "*ándale*," "*vámonos*" — each of the six men would give the nearest mule a slap, then let out a war whoop which was a "hang-on" signal to the passengers and away we would go! Ordinary speed was a cross-country runaway gallop, fast as the mules could go! On level stretches, or downhill, ruts, rocks, or short turns in the road meant nothing to mules or drivers. Obviously the main object of the mules was to get out of the way of that monster, the oncoming vehicle behind. Passing traffic, be it a bunch of sheep or a cow in the road, had better look out.

There may have been road laws in Mexico in 1895, but if so, nobody paid any attention. Along the one track wagon-way, the age-old custom of cutting brush and overhanging limbs with a *machete* (a broad, short sword) was still in practice, but rocks or ruts, anything a mule could not step over or jump, remained undisturbed. The road or trail went around such obstacles, and so did the mules and coach.

Topography, vegetation, scenery, and sights were much the same as in New Mexico: rolling hills, prairie-deserts flanked by mountain ranges, an occasional stream, grazing land, cattle and sheep. Circling buzzards (evidence of carrion), coyotes, jack rabbits, quail were plentiful, and at night, moon shadows of stumps, brush and cacti created imaginative suggestions of holdups.

To me, the sight of mysterious, solitary piles of loose stones alongside the road were strange. They were *mojoneros de muerte* (death mounds), reminders of a spot where somebody died, and the usual explanation given was ambush by bandits. Seldom did death come from natural causes. In after years this sight was common, yet it never lost its significance of human frailty, representing as it did a short-time reverence of those who built it. Some of the mounds were recent and some were old. Those of recent date were surmounted by a crude wooden cross, while the older ones were crumbled and neglected.

Our coach, quite customarily, was overloaded with baggage, mail, express and ten passengers, all of whom were Mexicans except myself. For the entire trip, on the seat facing me was a pros-perous-looking, fat and good-natured man, and at his waist, in a scabbard with the barrel protruding and pointing straight at me, was the biggest six-shooter I ever saw. Black coffee, the wild ride, and that big six-shooter left little inclination for sleep. The second day out the friendly fellow with the big gun inquired if I had slept during the night, and receiving a negative reply, he explained about the coffee, saying all the passengers were greatly surprised when they saw me fill my cup with the concentrated fluid. One thing I found about the Mexican people: they are polite and seldom intrude with suggestions unless requested to do so. We hung on somehow all day, all night, and the next day until 3:00 P.M. — thirty-six hours, 210 miles — at an average of 6 miles an hour including stops for meals and changing mules.

At last we reached Guanaceví, an old, well-known mining town where the influence of Spanish exploitation was still markedly apparent. Several thousand inhabitants were living in adobe houses built close together. The adobe houses lined the unpaved streets, but there were no sidewalks, no public utilities: only poverty everywhere. The town, as with most Spanish mining settlements, straddled a narrow, steep arroyo, through which ran a small dirty stream. This served as the main sewage disposal and refuse dump which, in season, was cleared sometimes by heavy rains and mountain freshets; yet, a constant and unavoidable stench remained.

The region roundabout was self-supporting in agriculture, rich in minerals and cattle, most of which were owned by one or two wealthy Spanish families who, for the most part, lived and spent their income elsewhere. It represented a region of Mexico as it was prior to 1900; yes, a hundred or two hundred years before. Because of its isolation, only a few Americans were then operating at or near Guanaceví, and those present were living in newly constructed quarters close to their own mine workings. The town sported no decent hotel or accommodations and living conditions were primitive. A Spanish vocabulary was imperative.

The compound provided by the company for its agent — me — consisted of a large common-style patio dwelling, situated on a side street near the center of town. It was an ancient, worn out, insect-infested residence and business place combined and had an old

*Guanacevi marketplace, where Parker's stay
and job as ore-buying agent were but short-lived.*

woman with three children acting as housekeeper. The patio was surrounded by flat-roofed one-story living quarters, with rooms and storage space for cargoes of ore. The ore was delivered by pack mules, unloaded, sampled, assayed and paid for; then it was re-sacked by the agent to be sent to the railroad at Jiménez by pack mule. Later the ore was shipped to the smelter at either El Paso[9] or Aguascalientes.[10] All help, neighbors, and associates were Mexican. The outlook for a future here I did not care to face! A glance, a bit of inquiry and recognition of conditions, was sufficient to convince me that the position of ore-purchasing agent in this locality was not for me, or mine. The young American whose place I was to take was in a hurry to return to the United States, but Lewis Brothers in Mexico City was advised by wire as to my decision. They had another man available, so an early exchange was possible with nobody hurt.

In future ventures, remembering Guanacevi, I was able to avoid too close personal contact with prevalent living conditions in Mexico, and while often located in places far from the railroad and along remote mountain trails, both living and working conditions were always under more recent development and more progressive operations.

My next trip into Mexico occurred in 1898 when I accepted an assignment from Britton Davis,[11] general manager of the Corralitos Land and Cattle Company, to examine an *antigua* (an ancient Spanish mine) in the southwestern part of the State of Chihuahua. This agreement resulted in a five-day journey by stage and muleback from the railroad into the heart of the Tarahumara Indian country.[12]

The first part of my journey was by train to Jiménez, which was the same route as my first trip into Mexico. Then, with Negro Tom as guide, we traveled 70 miles west to Parral[13] by Concord coach, using four relays of mules for the trip. Instead of the thirteen mules previously used, the Parral coach had nine which were less wild and better behaved. In comparison, the journey was pleasant enough, but somehow I missed the "big cannon" pointing constantly at my midriff!

At Parral we were warned against going into the Tarahumara country because Federal troops had but recently returned from there. This was a "sure sign" there had been trouble somewhere, though nobody seemed to know just what it was. All agreed, however, we would receive a hostile reception and advised strongly against our proceeding into that wild, isolated area. We decided to take the chance, but only because Negro Tom had been over the trail a month earlier. A mozo named Antonio was engaged, along with four mules, one for each of the three of us, and a pack animal to carry my roll of bedding and the grub box containing all the food and utensils and camping gear.

I carried my .38 caliber Smith and Wesson six-shooter, while on the horn of my saddle was tied a panorama Kodak in a leather case.[14] Tom carried a .44 Winchester rifle in a scabbard hung from the saddle, and the mozo was unarmed. The Mexican saddle such as we used is a *vicious* article because it was rough-hewn from a log of hardwood and had no padding. It was built ostensibly for the punishment of the rider! And punishment we took as we plodded one behind the other, up and down the narrow trails through the mountains, bucking the fierce, penetrating winds and February cold. Not one of us forgot for a minute the hostile area into which we were proceeding.

The third day out we crossed the Nonoava River,[15] usually a clear stream, but now swelled into a raging torrent. The pack mule, which was usually so surefooted and dependable, stepped into a hole and disappeared. Several hours were spent in a vain attempt to find the animal or at least a part of our luggage, but the mule, my bed roll, the grub box, dishes, cooking and eating utensils — all — were lost. Tom and I were down to a pocketknife apiece, but the mozo was just the same because he had nothing to lose. It was a sorry predicament, but we were within a day's journey of our destination, so naturally I wanted to go ahead. With night fast approaching, Tom mentioned a small Indian village[16] a few miles distant, so we decided to try it.

The village consisted of seven or eight thatch-roofed adobe shacks that were scattered among the brush at varying angles and distances apart. They were objects of extreme poverty. Our arrival was heralded by the barking of innumerable dogs as women and children scurried to their respective *jacales.* Fortunately one of the men spoke Spanish, so Tom and the mozo could "make talk," but it was apparent that they were not at all pleased to see us. Their greeting was cold and hostile, and they made repeated questions as to our business, particularly to see if we were buying cattle. It took some time to convince them of the purpose of our visit and the veracity of our story about the lost mule.

Having noticed a number of inquisitive, furtive glances toward the Kodak on my saddle, and thinking to appease their curiosity, I took it from its case and opened it, thus spoiling a film but showing an empty box. This led to explanations because they had never before seen a Kodak. Tom told me afterward that they thought it was a "money box."

Once convinced that our intentions were merely to visit the old Spanish mine nearby, they became friendly and invited us to remain overnight in the shack. There we ate a supper consisting of a thick porridge of roasted, ground peanuts served with goat's milk in a half gourd and eaten with a wooden spoon, and a piece of goat meat roasted on the end of a stick.

The family occupying the hut offered to sleep elsewhere and urged us to sleep inside, but upon seeing the evidence of vermin, I was grateful to note the diplomatic nonacceptance of Tom and his proposal that we go outside the village where our mules might get better pasturage. We camped that night in the open, undressing by taking off our shoes and sleeping with a saddle for a pillow and saddle blankets for cover against the cold.

Before going to sleep Tom asked how much silver money I had, explaining that we must not offer or show any paper money to these Indians. They had told him that several Mexican cowboys led by an American had recently purchased a bunch of cattle from them, for which they paid counterfeit paper money. The deceivers had driven the cattle off before the swindle was discovered, but the Indians' displeasure and lack of welcome to us was thus accounted for, and so was the Parral report about the Federal troops. Tom was delighted when I told him I had about seventy-five pesos in silver. He said: "That amount will keep us a month or two if we care to stay"— which, under the circumstances, emphatically I did not.

On returning to the village next morning we were served a meal similar to that of the night before, only this time "side-cakes" were added. The cakes consisted of peanuts which were roasted, ground, moistened, pressed into small cakes, and then fried in goat grease. Looking around we saw a number of bows and quivers stocked with arrows, belt knives and machetes, but, of firearms, not one. To satisfy our needs for the days ahead, several mules were brought in from which we selected one, also an *aparejo* (pack saddle) and a live goat, which we had them kill and dress. Also, for provisions on the trail, we purchased two gunnysacks full of peanuts for which they asked seventy-five centavos. I paid one peso ($.50 United States currency) and received their *muchas gracias,* but from Tom I got a reprimand for "spoiling the natives." "Pay 'em less, they like to haggle. Never, never pay 'em more. They respect you more when you tell 'em, not ask 'em."

We set out for the mine after settling the bill with silver, good news which spread rapidly among the natives. Thereafter we had no further trouble or special anxiety concerning them. Our destination proved to be a number of old roofless adobe buildings which were fast giving way to the elements, and the remains of an old smelter. The mine workings were filled with water below the 100-foot level. Of special note were the timbers used for support of all the accessible workings. It was of *hard wood,* a species quite plentiful in the neighborhood. To one side of the smelter was a good-sized slag dump, the unused tailings of ore refinement, which showed buckshot globules of lead and furnished evidence of a crude furnace and imperfect fusion. Alongside the slag was another dump, or pile, containing several hundred tons of practically pure litharge (oxide of lead — 90 percent plus, which meant that it was pure lead).

Instead of returning to Parral, a four-day journey, we headed north to the nearest provision point, San Borjas,[17] on the way to the well-known mining town of Cusihuiriachi (Cusi for short),[18] 75 miles west of the city of Chihuahua.[19] On this, our northward trek, the trail was along the Continental Divide, with the drainage sometimes toward the east and sometimes toward the west. It wound around the hills which were, in places, well timbered but had little underbrush. Good grazing was found only in the valleys, and campsites with water were few and far between.

There was a surprising lack of bird life or game, and only once, the day we left the antigua, did we see any deer. I saw the first, five or six of them straight ahead, a little to one side of the trail. I shot and missed, an act which caused a most disappointing moment! Tom was told to do the shooting next time, or let Antonio do it, but they never had a chance because we did not see another deer. We had no other opportunity to change our peanut diet!

As a break in the monotony of fairly horizontal travel the trail suddenly dropped into and across an upper section of the much publicized *Barranca del Cobre*.[20] What we saw was a modest replica of the *Fuerte Gorge*[21] farther down, of which the place we crossed is a part, yet the gorge we traversed was big and broad and deep enough to add more than half a day to our journey. We proceeded single file, but with uncertain confidence in the mule's superior judgment. At a spot in the trail wide enough to dismount without stepping into space, we got off to walk and found great relief from efforts of adjustment to the acute angles of that torture seat already described but bearing repetition: the saddle was still a block of hardwood, hand-carved, not designed for human fit nor comfort. No doubt about it, the Mexican saddle was a relic of the Inquisition from Spain.

Ten to fifteen miles west and almost paralleling our trail was another trail, wider and much more used. The two converged at Cusihuiriachi. It was the main supply and shipping route to the mining town and rich silver mines of Batopilas, a place doubly famous for its remarkable deposits of high-grade ore and the exceptional percentage of native pure silver, and also for the strange story of its owner, "Boss Shepherd" of Washington, D.C., an American who made good twice.[22]

During and following the Civil War, Shepherd was chairman of a committee appointed by Congress to redesign, expand, improve and beautify the city of Washington, D.C., in line with its importance and comparison with other world capitals. This was done as the plans were drawn to provide for streets, parks, and sites for buildings much as they are today. Political opposition and near-sighted economy caused Shepherd to be practically driven out of the city, and only in later years were the merits of his vision proved and his name extolled as the chief architect of the nation's capital. After leaving Washington he journeyed west across the plains by covered wagon and horseback to Santa Fe, thence south into Chihuahua to settle at Batopilas. There, with the passage of a few years, he became a millionaire several times over.

The trail we were on bypassed Batopilas a couple of days reaching that particular Cañon del Diablo, now known by the misnomer Barranca del Cobre, the name supposedly first applied by the intrepid prospectors who discovered Batopilas. An hour's ride beyond the barranca was a small village (less than a dozen *jacales*) and one L-shaped adobe with an enclosed patio. This structure was called *La Tiendita*, and it had an entrance door, a full length counter except for a passageway to the rear, shelves along the wall, and a door leading to the back room. Articles on display were few in number and small in quantity, representing the meagre necessities of daily consumption. Usually the store had only one gunnysack of each item. Corn, wheat, and peanuts made up the local seasonal produce, and added to this fare were coffee, pinoche sugar and sugarcane, crude rock salt which had been crushed, dry red chile hanging on a string, tobacco, cigarettes, garlic, lard in a tin can, perhaps a few tallow candles and two or more pint bottles of mescal.

Additional merchandise, if any, was kept out of sight, in the room back of the counter, or in another room of the patio or a separate house entirely, presumably for safety. Such precautions have to be taken owing to fear of roving bandits or neighborhood drunks, real or pretending government agents (inspectors and tax assessor-collectors), no small percentage of whom are all too intent on a "handout for protection." Scales for weighing are few and far between and small items are measured by hand-carved wooden spoons, half gourds from wild native vines, or sometimes by counting. The merchant, an elderly man or woman who is more thrifty perhaps than the others, is the community custodian or banker. Produce is brought to him in exchange for merchandise, and any surplus is shipped by him in exchange for outside requirements. Circulating cash is practically nil and that available is confined to copper centavos and *values* (IOUs which are issued verbally).

Glancing around the almost empty storeroom before leaving *La Tiendita,* I noticed on a high shelf, covered with thick dust, several familiar-shaped tin cans which on closer examination proved to be Armour's Corned Beef. The proprietor did not know what they were, where they came from, or how long he had had them. Cheerfully he sold the lot for one peso. With Tom as arbiter we probably would have paid only half that much since the peso to him was a national maximum! Along the trail a can was opened and because the meat was red, the mozo, Antonio, refused to eat it, saying it was horse meat and he preferred *carne seca* (dried goat meat) with his peanuts. We did not argue since he was satisfied and willing to go without, but to us it was a luxurious treat.

On we journeyed to San Borjas, a small town with an environment of rock fences and cultivated fields which provided a pleasing sight to weary travelers. It had no hotel, but like most towns in Mexico there was a tavern, a private dwelling owned and run by a widow, to which travelers were directed and for which we were grateful. We had eaten nothing but peanuts, goat meat, and a few small cans of corned beef for six full days, and we were starving for something else. The time we had to wait, probably not more than a couple of hours while our hostess and half a dozen other women prepared the meal, seemed endless. Need it be said that we ate everything available: boiled chicken, frijoles, queso (cheese), tortillas, two or three vegetables and coffee.

In order to fortify ourselves for the next day on the trail, an arrangement was made to have the tavern hostess kill, pluck, clean, cut up and oil six medium-sized chickens. The end of the sack was neatly tied in a knot. Dismounting, I thanked her and asked how much we owed. *"Seis reales,"* six bits, was the answer — seventy-five centavos. I gave her a peso and we started on our way after many friendly gestures, smiles, and further conversation consisting of *"Muchísimas gracias, adiós, Vaya con Dios."* But, immediately Tom was beside me and *mad.* "Mr. Parker," he said, "You just got to quit. You're spoiling these natives. Next time you come by here you'll be paying a peso apiece for them chickens." Of no significance at the time, but now fifty years later, is a marker in the comparison of the United States dollar and the Mexican peso: in 1897 six chickens cost one peso; exchange 50¢: 8.22¢ each. In 1947 Tom's prophecy was one chicken to cost one peso; exchange 12¢. I do not know the price of a chicken at San Borjas today, 1947, but my wager, if any, would be that it would cost less than in 1897.

When we lost our pack animal and all our possessions at the Conchos-Nonoava river crossing as related above, I was fortunate to find some tobacco and a pipe in the saddlebags on the mule I was riding. However, after a couple of days the desire to smoke was gone, and after two more days I could not smoke. Ever since that trip, whenever I have wanted to stop smoking, eating a five or ten cent bag of peanuts has proven it can be done.

Across and over the upper branches of the famed Barranca del Cobre was another of those volcanic-erosion chasms in the plateau of that region. Trail winding around the hills and over the flats, we used up two more days before reaching our muleback destination, the old mining town Cusihuiriachi, a terminal of a stagecoach line from Chihuahua City. A few years later the two towns were connected by rail, but at that time the stage line was the primary means of transportation.[23]

Cusi was an unlovely old mining town situated on one side of the hill near the upper end of a long valley. It had but one main street on which the stores and principal buildings were close together. Homes of the mine workmen were spread all over the landscape, and for the most part they were mere jacales, hovels, and huts. The hillsides roundabout for miles were stripped of all trees and shrubs, the result of longtime exploitation. Several thousand persons lived here, few of whom were Americans, but there were no public schools, no playgrounds for children, no libraries or hospitals. Here we rested a couple of days, long enough for a hot bath, with soap, a shave in a barbershop and the purchase of a toothbrush, clean underwear, shirt and socks.

From Cusi the mules and aparejos were sent back to Parral with our mozo, Antonio, a trusted friend of the owner, in charge. In exchange for the mule lost in crossing the Conchos-Nonoava River, we sent the one purchased from the Tarahumaras. A 20-mile wagon road led north from Cusi to a station, San Antonio,[24] about midway on the branch railway from Chihuahua City west to the terminus at Miñaca.[25] The light coach in which we covered this short distance was a welcome relief from the back of a mule and a hardwood Mexican saddle. The journey from Cusi into Chihuahua City was made in a Concord stagecoach drawn by six large American horses that had been grain- and hay-fed and were similar to those north of the border, and with which I had long been familiar. Almost the entire distance was upon and across a portion of the Terrazas six million-plus acre ranch.[26]

The days were temperate and sunshiny, with a bright moon at night, and the ever-changing landscape revealed undulating hills and broad valleys, wooded sections of scrub oak and cedar, juniper and piñon trees, cottonwoods along the streambeds, yucca and other cacti, mesquite and sagebrush. The whole scene was blanketed with verdant, nutritious harvest grama and red-top grass, and, as far as the eye could see, slick, fat, contented cattle, horses, mules and sheep. The saying was in reality true: "The owner himself did not know how many; the branding of 50,000 calves annually was not uncommon." For the year 1910, when the Madero revolution[27] started, this figure was nearly doubled. Authenticity for the last two sentences is Don Juan Terrazas,[28] son of the old man Don Luis, then living in El Paso and with whom I was well acquainted.

From Chihuahua to Juárez and El Paso by train was 250 miles, and the trip was a joy and pleasure deluxe because it offered a break in the monotony of travel. It had rail for a trail, an engine for a mule, a cushion for a saddle! I was home at last and found everybody well. My second trip to Mexico was happily ended. My report on the antigua was unfavorable, a recommendation based on the paucity of labor and supplies, the low grade of the ores, and the region's inaccessibility. This report, made to Britton Davis, general manager, was followed by my appointment as Underground Mine Superintendent at Minas de San Pedro.

Parker's 1898 Trip into Mexico

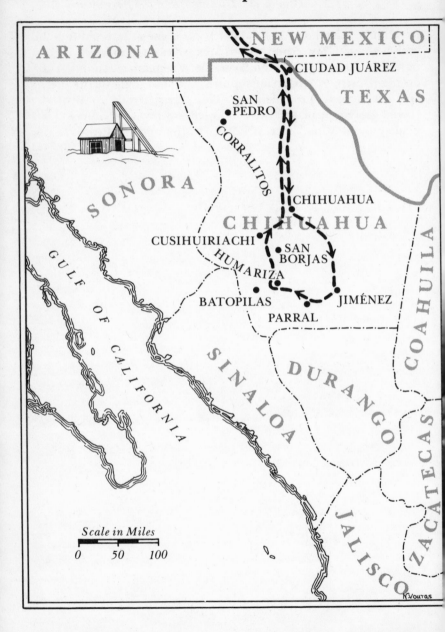

Corralitos and
Minas de San Pedro, Chihuahua

IN 1886, WHILE THE SANTA FE RAILROAD was building south toward Mexico City, a group of New York financiers headed by E. D. Morgan[1] (cousin of J. Pierpont) purchased a one-million-acre property approximately 125 miles south of El Paso. It was an old Spanish land grant called "El Rancho de Corralitos"[2] and consisted of an area 25 percent larger than the state of Rhode Island. The men were willing to take a chance because the political regime of Porfirio Díaz was encouraging the influx of foreign capital.[3] This investment was representative of others which followed, a trend that continued until 1911 when Díaz lost control.

In close proximity to the Corralitos were other ranches of equal or greater acreage. To the south was the W. R. Hearst ranch,[4] to the west was the Beresford,[5] to the northwest was the Boyd,[6] to the north was the two-million-acre Palomas,[7] and to the east was the Terrazas with six million, an area 10 percent larger than Massachusetts.

As implied, the time of acquisition, with the exception of the Terrazas holdings, coincided with the first all-out expression of United States confidence in the stability of the Mexican government under President Don Porfirio Díaz. Thenceforth, invited and encouraged by the latter, foreign capital entered the enticing field of opportunities there offered. Gaining momentum, the last fifteen years of Díaz's regime, 1895–1910, proved the most progressive and prosperous in the history of the nation. More than

$1.5 billion was invested in Mexico, and over $1 billion of that was American capital.

General Manager at Corralitos for some twenty years, 1886–1906, was Britton Davis, an ex-lieutenant of the Third United States Cavalry, which, during the early 1880s, was a leading unit of United States forces engaged in the pacification and control of the Apache and other Indians in the territories of New Mexico and Arizona. They were also active in chasing the notorious Geronimo across the border. In connection with the latter, as leader of his platoon near Corralitos, Lieutenant Davis chanced to meet the group of New York financiers who had recently purchased the land. They saw in Davis the manager they needed because he was a man of excellent physique, had an outstanding personality, and spoke fluent Spanish. He was fairly conversant with cattle and a qualified Indian fighter — all in all a man capable of conducting and protecting their interests.

E. C. Houghton,[8] an experienced cattleman, was given the supervision of the ranching activity which became one of the finest in Mexico. The inferior big-boned Mexican longhorns were replaced with white-faced Herefords, the entire million acres was fenced with barbed wire, and cross fences were added to provide separate pastures for breeding, market stock, bulls, and horses. Because of these improvements and superior facilities, the ranch became distinctive throughout the Southwest.

The Beresford ranch[9] adjoining west of Corralitos was owned by Lord Delaval Beresford,[10] a brother of Sir Charles, an admiral in the British Navy. The story was told that his family opposed his marriage to an English girl of his choice because she was not of the nobility. She subsequently married, perhaps by force, another man, and in retaliation Delaval Beresford left England for America, where he endeavored to drink all the liquor in the country. During a serious illness in a Southern home or hospital, he was nursed by a Negress, Lady Flo,[11] whom he subsequently married — common-law or legal?

Tall, slender, ungainly, no curves, Lady Flo became well known and proved to be an acknowledged worthy helpmate for her companion. Her business acumen was as good as or better than his, and, since she was customarily consulted in all important deals, she was credited with rescuing him from many financial pitfalls. The Beresford ranch was noted for its hospitality because Don, or Lord, Delaval had many friends and entertained lavishly. Lady Flo was a fine cook. People say they often fought like cats and dogs, but that Lady Flo was the usual victor. She was the acknowledged "Boss" of the ranch, rode horseback wherever he did, and often traveled with him on journeys to the United States and Mexico City, dressed in the best clothes that money could buy: silks and satins, hats from Paris, diamonds, and furs.

He never denied their relationship. Whenever he had one of his drinking "spells" which went beyond control, it was for Lady Flo he called — no one else could do anything for or with him. They lived together for many years until his death in a railway accident near Medicine Hat, Alberta, Canada.[12] Sir Charles sent agents from England who somehow contrived by paying her a pension and lump sum of money to gain title to the ranch, which was afterward sold.

Embraced within the boundaries of the Corralitos property, but at the time of purchase of doubtful merit were some antigua Spanish mines known as Minas de San Pedro,[13] situated 16 miles east of Corralitos. Under Davis's management, renewed activity in this area resulted in the reopening of two or three old mines and the discovery of others. A local smelting plant was built and fair profits were made for several years; however, increasing costs of fuel for the smelter and transportation to and from the railroad which was 90 miles to the east eventually diminished the profits. The company also wanted to cut costs on cattle shipping, so it built its own railroad, the Río Grande, Sierra Madre and Pacific, from Juárez to Casas Grandes, a distance of 115 miles.[14] Thus under the same ownership were the ranch, mines, and railroad.

"Corralitos," the hacienda-village typical of earlier day Spanish administration, was situated in the Casas Grandes valley near the east bank of the Corralitos River. The main street, about 100 feet wide and ½ mile long, was bordered on both sides with immense, wide-spreading cottonwood trees. Iron rings 6 inches in diameter were embedded in the bark so deeply that only the outer rim was visible, a curiosity which added greatly to the evidence of age. They had been placed there originally for tethering the horses of visiting caballeros, and, where exposed in 1898, were still used for that same purpose.

The principal building was the hacienda proper, one story in height, one room in width and a succession of adjacent rooms surrounding an enclosed patio of about an acre of ground, 200 feet to a side. The walls were massive, of adobe 4 to 6 feet thick, and

The main street of Corralitos, Chihuahua,
a hacienda-village on a 1-million acre land grant
managed by Britton Davis. The hacienda-village was
typical of early-day Spanish administration.

the outer windows were all wood (no glass) with peek-hole shutters and iron bars. The roof was flat, with drainage projections of hollowed half logs, while the outer walls extended as a breastwork 3 to 4 feet above the roof in an effort to provide protection against attack.

Doors inside the patio afforded entrances to all the rooms which served as living quarters for the owner, his household servants and guards. Also within this enclosure were warehouses for grain, beans, dried fruit, meat, leather and wool, a blacksmith shop, a carpenter shop, an area for making saddles, aparejos, *riatas* (lariats, ropes), and space for carding wool, making blankets and cloth, a plant for making sugar, an *arrastra* for treatment of high-grade gold and silver ores. All of this represented the industrialization of the old-time haciendas.

The village itself consisted of a continuation of similar squares (city blocks) and patios. Houses joined each other and each had a front entrance on the street and rear patio. The dwellings were sufficient in number to accommodate approximately one thousand people.

The river ran north across the ranch, emptying into a broad shallow basin, Lake Guzmán,[15] before it reached the border. Along its banks were a number of communal settlements and farms. All persons inside the boundary of the ranch were employees and tenants of the owner.

The name Minas de San Pedro was derived from the oldest and largest of the antigua workings, which boasted records antedating A.D. 1750. The San Pedro was a fair example of old Spanish mine operations. The ore shoot had been worked out long before the advent of the Americans. Without machinery or mechanical equipment of any kind, using black powder, unslaked lime, and fire as explosives to break out the ore, the Spaniards had mined approximately 40,000 tons of solid ore and rock from this area which was 450 feet deep and 400 feet along the vein. This activity had required more than one million loads which were packed out on the backs of workers, each load averaging about seventy-five

San Pedro Mine, 16 miles east of Corralitos, a fair example of old Spanish mining operations. Parker was made underground superintendent in 1898. The mine entrance (lower right) is 900 feet above the valley floor.

pounds. In addition, several times that number of round trips had been necessary to carry out in water skins the ever constant underground flow of water.

The workings, abandoned, filled with water. A number of years before our arrival someone had driven a cross-cut tunnel 900 feet long, with the object, no doubt, of draining the water in order to examine the lower workings. The stoped area [16] was encountered, but nothing of commercial value was found; the ore shoot had been exhausted to its outermost limits. After that time, the mine was again abandoned, and but little additional work was done. Scouting around in old drifts and from the broken material below the adit, [17] we found several short, round, cast-iron pointed tools, probably chisels, which were used by the old-time miners, probably as drills and wedges.

High on the hillslope above the drainage tunnel mentioned, was the one and only entrance to the old mine workings. A short passageway led to an underground chapel about 25 feet long, 13 feet wide, and 6 to 7 feet high, cut from the solid vein and rock walls. Along both sides and on one end, the rock near the floor was left in place to serve as seats, while at the other end was a higher platform which served as an altar. Placed upon the altar and in cut niches of the wall around the room were various objects of worship including a mixture of candles, flowers, and an assortment of glass containers and clay pots.

During our sojourn at San Pedro, while services were held elsewhere to accommodate the larger attendance, the underground chapel remained a sacred place of worship and on special days services were conducted therein. The audience, too numerous for the space inside, gathered on the hillslope and around the open cut, where, from a vantage point, the priest would deliver his message and extend his blessings.

Elsewhere in Mexico and in all of our mines at San Pedro, at no very great distance below the surface, were to be found similar, though smaller, shrines. A short drift, an abandoned station, an excavation alongside the ladderway served this function as candles and flowers, fresh and artificial, were replaced and candles lit, if necessary, by the first man going on shift, day or night. As the miners passed, each gave the customary salutation and crossed himself in reverence.

Opposite the entrance to the San Pedro chapel and leading therefrom was another and smaller opening to the large stoped area below. By means of these two openings, both of which passed through the church, all the rock and ore was brought to the surface packed on the backs of men. Fiber or cowhide sacks were used for the ore and pigskin bags served as water containers. To hold the load in place and assist in carrying, each bag had a short handlestrap three inches wide which was fastened to opposite top edges of the bag. In carrying the load, the strap was placed across the man's forehead, thus allowing both feet and hands free for use in climbing. The incline slope, sixty to seventy degrees from horizontal, was not only steep but slippery; a misstep or slip was usually fatal.

Light underground was supplied by *mechas* (torches) ranging up to two and a half inches in diameter and being thirty-six inches long. They were made of tallow and hemp which was pounded together and pressed in long narrow split pieces of wood and then bound with fibers of maguey or other cactus. Not carried by the workmen, but placed at intervals along the inclined slopes and ladderways, the men groped their way between. Even with the utmost economy in their use, the smoke and ventilation must have been worse than awful. As the stope area increased horizontally along the vein, openings were made to the surface for ventilation which, assisted by fires near the surface, caused an updraft suction from below. That such openings were intended or used for no other purpose is evidenced by the small size of the rock piles (dumps) near their entrance.

With us, even though we had good lights to explore the limits of the stope, to ascend or descend the steep slope was a precarious, dangerous undertaking. A clear head, steady nerve, exact equilibrium and body balance were vitally essential. It was no place for a novice.

My entrance into the picture occurred in 1898, a few months before the completion of the railroad and after my return from the Tarahumara Indian country. As previously mentioned it was for Britton Davis that the Tarahumara examination was made, with a half promise on his part, and hopes on mine, that it might lead to something better.

After reading the report, and listening to my application for continued service, he explained the situation: the mine production at Minas de San Pedro, which had been slipping for some time, was then 90,000 pesos ($45,000.00) in the red; the railroad was dubious, the ranch doing fairly well. The New York directors had become increasingly critical of using profits from the ranch to keep the mines going, "tired of throwing cattle down the shafts!" A newly appointed superintendent of operations had doubtful experience underground. An opening was possible. In brief, I was offered the dubious task of making the mines pay dividends; I was given a six-month trial provided after investigation I believed I could pay expenses from production.

In reference to my confession of weakness — the language — Mr. Davis retorted, "A handicap, yes, but not serious. Let their politics alone, let their religion alone, let their women alone, and you will have no difficulty." Excellent business advice in any man's country!

In the change of management at the mines made a few weeks earlier, D. Bruce Smith,[18] an energetic and capable Scotsman had been engaged as superintendent. Formerly with the American Smelting and Refining Company smelter at Zacatecas,[19] his knowledge of mining was largely confined to reduction of ores rather than production. He was affable, agreeable and optimistic, and between us the position was divided: Smith as surface superintendent, myself as underground. Each in his particular sphere, the work was coordinated; we worked together without friction and remained lifelong friends.

On my preliminary visit, one of the outstanding things noted was the overcrowded conditions under which the miners (drillers) were working in the various stopes, thus retarding efficiency. It was a clear case of attempting to force production beyond development, and that is always a mistake where uniform output is essential. With my little hand pick and sample bags, and a "nose for ore," samples were painstakingly chipped from the vein along the various levels and other exposed working places in search of prospective and more promising places in which to work. Sufficient evidence was found to modify or reverse immediately the policy and methods then prevailing. Half or more of the men in the stopes were put to work extending the faces of drifts and making connections between levels, upraising and sinking winzes.[20] Results were quickly apparent. More ore was produced at the same time that new ground was explored, then developed for other and more extensive stoping.

Using nerve and good luck, profits from mine operations approximated $1 million annually within eighteen months. By the end of the fiscal year, some six months after I first saw the mines, the deficit was wiped out and a $10,000 profit balance shown. From that time on, talk about closing down the mines was forgotten, "no more cattle went down the mine," since profits exceeded those from the ranch!

Without going into details, suffice it to say that by the end of the first year the properties were in condition to assure profits for an indefinite period. New discoveries and development necessitated a branch spur to the main line of the railroad, 3 miles south of the first, leading to the Congreso-León[21] carbonate deposits of lead, silver, and gold, which in due course equalled, then exceeded, the output of the Candelaria, the largest and richest sulphide mine of the district.[22] Two trainloads of ore each day was our normal production. The Candelaria Mining Company became the largest and most profitable producer of northern Mexico.[23] The various mines were in an area about 3 miles long and half that wide. When we first went to Minas de San Pedro in March 1898, there were only two so-called camps, or villages. One, the original old Spanish

*The Congreso-León Mine, yielding lead, silver, and gold.
It eventually became the largest tonnage producer of them all.*

*The Candelaria Mine, one of the only two so-called mining camps
operating when Parker arrived on the scene in 1898.
Candelaria was the largest and richest sulphide mine of the district.*

settlement of San Pedro, established about 1750, had rows of flat-roofed adobe houses built close together, a large company ware-house and store combined, and a jail, an old abandoned mine tunnel with an iron-bar door and extra-heavy padlock. The other camp, Candelaria, was all American and more recently constructed. It had large adobe combination office-warehouse rooms for bache-lors, a restaurant, and a score or more of dwellings for officials and their families.

The two camps, about a mile apart, were separated by a high east-west ridge; San Pedro to the north, Candelaria to the south. About equidistant from the crest of this ridge, on either side and parallel about 500 feet apart, were two strong fissure veins from which were mined the greatest tonnage and richest sulphide ores in the district: silver, copper, lead, zinc, and gold. Later, a third camp was established about a mile southwest of Candelaria, near the San Nicolás-Cobriza sulphide mines, and still later, another, a fourth, was founded about a mile south of San Nicolás. This last one, the Congreso-León, yielded carbonate-oxide ores — lead, silver, and gold — and it eventually became the largest tonnage producer of them all.

This distinctive contrast of sulphide and oxide was a boon for both the producer and the smelter. The smelter penalty charges for treatment of sulphide ores was offset, in part at least, by pre-mium allowances on the oxides, since the latter were necessary for flux and smelting of the sulphides.[24] As the work increased and labor was none too plentiful, the old smelter patio and buildings were fixed up and used to accommodate 100 or more Chinese. Rice and dried fish were their main diet, and the odor resulting therefrom was evidence of locality and nationality. Being recent immigrants, only a few of them spoke either Spanish or English, so a boss interpreter was necessary and a secondary boss was assigned to each working group.

At first, the number of Americans employed, surface and under-ground, was possibly twelve; the number of mines working, four: Candelaria, Durita, San Nicolás, Congreso. Three years later

The San Nicolás sulphide mine, one of twenty-odd San Pedro mines in a 1½- by 3-mile strip.

twenty-odd producing mines were on my list, nine of which were of major importance with the balance being "prospects" of lesser production. Major properties each had an American foreman, shift and level bosses, and a timekeeper, and also contractors where speed on shaft work, drifts and raises was important.

Eventually, at peak production, the population of all four camps approximated 5000, and the number of laborers was more than 1000. The labor turnover was 200 or 300 percent, which means that with 1000 employed daily, the payroll contained 2000 to 3000 names due to changing from one mine to another, drunks after payday, or layoffs to visit friends and relatives.

When the supply of labor from local sources became acute, family importation was the answer. An agency was established at Zacatecas, a large mining center farther south on the Mexican Central Railroad, from where, at intervals as required, carloads of miners and their families were brought in, the company, of course, paying the freight. Long rows of two-room houses, each one with a fireplace, were built, and wages nearly double those at

Zacatecas were paid. Unfriendly association was minimized and competition as rival miners augmented. Everybody was satisfied.

As each and every one of the old workings was entered and examined by me, some to be sampled to determine if they might show any prospective values, I became sufficiently familiar with the sad plight of human poverty and degradation. Close contact with trash, rubbish, and filth, mixed with piles and scattered branches of thick-pronged cacti brought in by trade rats was such that, on returning home, knowing I would be denied entrance otherwise, and, more perhaps as a matter of self-preservation, I found it necessary to completely disrobe outside in the backyard. In a washtub with hot water and soap, I would scour and scrape and rinse to de-odorize, de-verminize, and de-insectize. Fleas, millions of fleas, were the most apparent and least odorous plague. Hat, clothes, and shoes were hung on a line outside the yard fence for old Chew (the house boy) to squirt flea powder on, brush, and clean.

The Chinese, constantly increasing in number, were a big help.[25] Landing at points along the west coast, they infiltrated inland seeking employment or an agricultural field on which to settle. They were welcomed as laborers because of their dependability, so a separate camp for the Chinese workmen was provided. They were especially good at sorting ore, which is the process of separating the pay ore from the waste rock and the low-grade ore.

At one time during a labor shortage period, the San Nicolás mine was worked entirely with Chinese labor, except foreman, shift, and level bosses. It required about seventy-five Chinese. About the time they became accustomed to drill, hammer, and shovel, the shortage ended and so did the underground work for Chinese.

Life at
Minas de San Pedro

WE REMAINED AT MINAS DE SAN PEDRO for four-and-one-half years. They were happy years with many pleasant memories with Genevieve, my wife,[1] but there were occasional jolts which were not so pleasant. As I recall, when I first went to San Pedro there was only one American woman in camp, Mrs. Stovall, wife of the company doctor.[2] Mr. Smith, the superintendent, was then a bachelor, but was married about a year later to Gertrude Winsor, daughter of an English widow at El Paso.[3] As the mines developed, more houses were built and other American families came in.

Genevieve, with baby Lina, came down from White Oaks, New Mexico, our former home. For the 90-mile stagecoach ride from White Oaks to the railroad, a large laundry clothes basket provided a comfortable cushion for Lina, who was placed on the floor of the coach and later between seats on the train when she was not held in her mother's or somebody else's arms.

We were allotted the ex-superintendent's residence, a glass brick one-story house, of seven rooms, double-L or U shaped. There were three rooms across the front and two back at each end. The glass bricks had been made by pouring slag from the old smelter into molds. On account of iron in the ore, they were jet black like obsidian (volcanic glass) and were very heavy. When set in lime mortar or cement, they were strong and durable, warm in winter and cool in summer.

Ours was the largest of several similar glass structures. The rough board floors were covered with heavy woolen rugs made in square patterns of a distinctive type, handwoven by native Indian-Mexicans at Corralitos who were noted for such work. The wool was sheared from their own sheep, cleaned, carded, and woven with geometrical designs in ancient looms. The material was colored by mineral or vegetable dyes known to the Indians long before Cortez.

During our first summer (1898) at San Pedro there occurred a violent epidemic of smallpox. We perceived that the attitude of the Mexicans was that, as dreaded as the disease was, nothing could be done about it. Quarantine and vaccination were either unknown or not practiced. God willing, the patient recovered; otherwise not. The epidemic was particularly prevalent and fatal among the children.

One day in climbing down the ladder in a winze of the Candelaria mine where two Mexican miners were at work I noticed the air was unusually close, murky, damp, and hot. Neither of the men wore a shirt or pants, merely a G-string and sandals. A quick look, and immediately I was off for a record on climbing a seventy-five foot ladder. One of the men's face and body was a mass of scabs, peeling blotches, and healing smallpox sores, the very worst stage for contagion. Luckily, I had been vaccinated. I hurried home, took a scalding hot bath in the patio outside the house, hung all my clothes on a line for several days, and suffered no ill effects.

As yet, the epidemic had not, to our knowledge, spread to the Americans in camp, but within a few days, Genevieve with little Lina went to call on the wife of the assistant store manager, a young man named Smith whose father had recently been sent from New York as auditor for the company headquarters office at El Paso. Mrs. Smith was in bed with a high fever. Lina was placed on the bed beside her, remaining there playing until time to go home. Next morning the doctor reported Mrs. Smith down with smallpox, contracted, he thought, by handling worn paper money at the store in helping her husband sort it into piles of like denomination. The best place for Genevieve and Lina, we decided, would be at the ranch with her mother at Carrizozo, near White Oaks, New Mexico.

For house help, we had in succession several maids from Colonia Dublan,[4] one of the Mormon colonies recently established near Casas Grandes, 10 miles south of Corralitos. The first girl, in answer to Genevieve's question, "How many in your family?" replied, "I am one of 34 children." We do not recall how many wives she said her father had. After about one month's training she quit to go home to get married.

The second girl, after a somewhat similar period, developed indications that her mind was in the same groove! When she asked my wife in all seriousness if she objected to her husband having more than one wife, the maid left the next day! Industrious though they were, one after another of the maids quit to be married about the time they began to show signs of helping instead of increasing the work.

This procedure of paying for the privilege of teaching a graduate course in home economics in time lost its charm, and was replaced by one wherein there was no marriage complex. With a group of intelligent clean-looking Chinese working around camp, the solution to this problem was found. A young, happy-faced boy recently arrived from China was selected. Proud of his new position and eager to learn, Sing made good.

In addition to our Chinese servant, Sing, we selected as a chore-boy and helper, a memorable character named Old Chew. Too old for work around the mines but eager to please in everything he did or was told to do, he was a dependable old fellow, strictly honest, frugal and economical to the nth degree, with his greatest anxiety being *waste*. We remembered him for his kindly smile and willing disposition. He slept in one of the back rooms used principally for junk and storing provisions, and he ate scraps from the kitchen in preference to regular portions. When a chicken was killed for the table, instead of wringing or chopping its head off and allowing it to flop all over the place, Chew slit its throat with a knife, let the blood drip into a cup and drank the blood.

He saved for himself the head, legs, and entrails, which he cleansed and cooked in an iron pot in the fireplace in his room where he ate the lot, disdaining completely what we considered the edible portion unless it was to be thrown out.

When our second and third babies were born, the first thing Old Chew wanted to know was whether they were boys. Both times I answered "No, another little girl," and both times he repeated over and over, "Ah, too bad, too bad." With our second baby, Frances, before she could walk and for some time afterward, Old Chew would carry her outside the house using one hand for a seat and positioning the other to hold her upright. He patiently paced back and forth for hours and miles. He spoke practically no English or Spanish, and what little of either he knew were mostly swearwords. He cooed, sang and talked to her in Chinese. At two years of age she understood Old Chew as well as she did her mother, but her conversation was a mixture of strange expressions with a surprising fringe of swearwords, some of which we could understand.

Her mixed language continued for some time after we left San Pedro. At two-and-a-half years, when visiting the home ranch at Carrizozo, New Mexico, Hodo, the cook, had placed her on the kitchen table so she could watch him kneading bread. Absorbed in his work, he paid no attention to the exclamation, *"Bájame"* (Let me down). Not understanding, he ignored the demand. Soon the call was repeated, only louder and more abruptly, *"Baja, baja, tu old sons-a-bichen, bájame."* Hodo never had a bigger jolt, nor a bigger laugh. Later, when questioned by her grandmother, Mrs. McDonald, as to why she had scolded Hodo with awful words, Frances replied, "I diddy know his other name." Hodo, old-time Indian scout, cowboy, and chuck-wagon cook, told that story repeatedly, as long as he lived. The last time we heard it was on a visit to the Soldiers' Home at Sawtelle, California, years later, where he spent his last remaining days.

Old Chew was with us about three years, until we left San Pedro. His wages were thirty pesos ($15.00) a month. When I say he was sixty years old I mean sixty plus; if he knew, he never would tell. A couple of months after he came to work at the house, he brought what money he had and asked me to keep it for him. He never gambled, or cared to do what so many did — send money back home to the bank at Hong Kong by means of a draft from El Paso. Explanations were of no avail, so I finally told him that I would not only take care of his money, but I would put it in the bank where it would draw interest.

Each month, thereafter, he received his thirty pesos and kept it overnight. Then he would bring it to me and ask that I put it with his other money. After several months passed, we suddenly noticed a change. For several days we noticed that Old Chew was not himself; he was grouchy, unwilling, simply impossible. I cornered and questioned him. He wanted his money, and I supposed he was going to quit. Instead of delaying by sending to the bank in El Paso, I simply drew the amount, plus interest, from the company safe, leaving my IOU therefor, and gave it to him. His eyes beamed and he salaamed until his head almost touched the floor.

Later that same day I called in the Chinese boss-interpreter, told him about the change in Old Chew and suggested he find us another servant. In answer he said, "Don't worry. Chew is all right. He'll be back in a day or two. Some of the other Chinamen, especially the gamblers, told Chew that now he did not have any money, that he had given it back to you, that it was now yours and he would never get it back." Sure enough, the next day before breakfast Chew came bringing his money in two separate packages. He said: "Too much money, too much." He handed me one of the packages, saying "Not my money, too much." Again I explained about the interest, but he would have none of it.

Thrusting the other package into my hands, he said: "You keep. I be good now." Then he turned and went back to his work, more cheerful and happier than ever. All he wanted was to see his money, to feel it, count it, sleep with it; one night apparently was long enough.

Every few months thereafter this same thing occurred. Chew simply went haywire, became cross, and was no good. I would go to the safe, draw out his money plus the interest, and give it to him. The next day, invariably he was back with two packages, his money in one, the interest in the other, and would say "too much money." He never could understand about interest.

Finally, when we were about to leave San Pedro, Chew told us he was going home to China. The amount was now more than one thousand pesos. All the time he was with us he spent practically nothing because he wore my old clothes, and shoes. He had already told us he had a wife and family in China. Now, he would be a rich man over there since three pesos a month was good money for one family. In reply to my question how he intended to transfer the money, he said he would carry it himself in a belt sewed around his waist. When I cautioned him that someone might steal it, even kill him if they suspected he was carrying money, he said: "Go with other old man-friend — I sleep, he watch; he sleep, I watch — good friend, good man." In reply to my question as to how he intended to go home, he said in broken lingo, "Uncle Sam, he send me home."

What he referred to was the policy of the Chinese to cross the border anywhere and get caught, then "Uncle Sam" would deport them free to China. Accommodations furnished free by Uncle Sam were far superior to those for which they would pay the steamship company! Whether or not Old Chew got home we never knew.

The Big Time at Corralitos was the week-long, annual fiesta, when the governor of the state, Don Miguel Ahumada,[5] with a select number of his merry aides and the state military band, came from Chihuahua City to help celebrate. The band was rated second best to that of Mexico City, one of the finest in North America. Our manager, Britton Davis, and the governor were a congenial pair: both military men, tall, fine-looking; Davis, light-complexioned, the governor, dark. Both were in their prime and knew good society, good wine, and how to entertain. The spacious hacienda provided ample accommodations. One feature of its furnishings, used only on such occasions, was a china cabinet along the entire end of one room which contained quantities of beautiful cut glass, crystal, and silverware used only for banquet service.

Under the conditions and environment, this was a sight even for *trained* eyes to see.

People flocked from all the surrounding country, the population far overflowing all resident accommodations. Among the attractions were the never absent itinerant circus, merry-go-round, acrobats; food and curio stalls, tables for outdoor gambling, card games, big and little shell games, rings and balls for pitching and throwing chances; anything and everything to magnetize the natives and separate them from their savings.

Horse racing was, of course, the main daylight excitement. Corralitos prided itself on its breed of horses, and neighboring ranches were not slow in disputing their time and distance. Rodeos, bronco "busting," lassoing, time-count for roping, tying wild steers, fancy riding and rope work, filled in the time between races. It was all filled with color, excitement, and fun!

As circumstances permitted, our principal diversion was the hunting of deer, duck, quail, and dove. In the surrounding hills at no great distance, big blacktail deer were plentiful; wild ducks by the thousands were easy prey — the Corralitos River 16 miles west, the Santa María[6] the same east, with numerous sloughs and ponds. Shooting ducks along the railroad was no novel exploit since it was engaged in daily by the engineer, conductor, train crew and passengers. Excavations alongside the tracks, in season filled by the rains, made ideal resting places for the migratory birds. With no important schedule necessary to maintain, frequent stops allowed time for the hunters, spaced a few feet apart, to walk forward on the side opposite the swimming ducks, then, at a pre-arranged signal in unison crawl to the top of the embankment and shoot. The bag of a dozen or more ducks was not infrequent.

A first class tennis court was laid out so that single games and local tournaments could be played. Included in the Candelaria campsite was a stable and corral for company mules and horses. There the saddle horses for Mr. Smith, the doctor, and myself were kept and cared for. Each morning the boy brought them to our respective houses and came after them at night. For special use we had a *carruaje,* a three-seated, light covered wagon drawn by four large American mules and driven by Black Tom, the corral boss. This we used on hunting trips when we expected to be gone overnight, our saddle horses trailing behind, led by one of the corral mozos.

The memory of things not so pleasant still remains vivid. About a mile from where we lived, on the flat and near the road leading to the Congreso Mine, an American named Friend owned and was working a small lead and silver mine. Nearby were several tent-houses for workmen, in one of which his family, a wife and three small children, lived. We were at home eating lunch one day when he rode up on horseback all excited, and said that one of his children had been struck by a rattlesnake. Mounting my horse which was always tethered and saddled in front of the house, we rushed to get Dr. Stovall. Then all three of us hurried as fast as possible to his camp. His three-year-old girl had been struck just below the ear in the cords of her throat, a direct strike with all the venom forced into her system. The little one was already turning black, in great pain, suffering terribly. The doctor did everything possible, which was not much on account of the dangerous and vital spot of the reptile's lunge. Within an hour of our arrival she passed away, the entire upper portion of her body black as if she were Negro.

The mother told us the story: The children were playing in the sagebrush not more than a hundred feet from the house when she heard them scream. She rushed out to where the children were running toward her. It seems the little girl, seeing the snake crawling in the brush, had reached down to pick it up, apparently as a plaything. Before her older sister could intervene the snake coiled and struck. Rushing to where the attack occurred, the mother saw and killed the snake, and immediately the father was notified. Owing to the delay in catching and saddling his horse, a full hour or more elapsed before the doctor arrived, but the doctor stated: "Even had I been present when the snake struck, I doubt anything I could do would have saved the child's life." It is known the amount of poison venom discharged from the fangs of a diamondback rattler the first time he strikes may be as much as two full tablespoons.

Supt. D. B. Smith and family lived in an adobe house which was about a city block from us. In the rear was a small yard enclosed by a four-foot adobe fence. A middle-aged Mexican woman was engaged as a full-time nurse for the baby who was about one year old. The nurse, who had been with them for several months, apparently had their complete confidence.

It happened on a Sunday when almost all the Americans were on a picnic several miles from camp. My wife, Genevieve, was by herself at home when a couple of Mexican women, excited and waving their arms, came running with the news that something out of the ordinary was taking place at the Smith house. At mention of the words *niñita*, *chiquita*, *infante*, the meaning cleared somewhat. Hurriedly she accompanied the women to the Smith residence where, on entering the back patio, they found the nurse lying in a pool of blood with a knife blade in her chest. The baby, with her little hands and dress covered with blood, was nudging and caressing the now quiet form. Without hesitation Genevieve picked up the baby, carried her home, bathed and redressed her in our own baby Lina's clothes, and awaited the arrival of her parents several hours later.

Both Mr. and Mrs. Smith were at the picnic. The office was notified, the *comisario* (chief of police) called, and a messenger sent to notify the Smiths. According to law, the body was left where it lay until the police from Casas Grandes arrived the next morning. After investigation, the verdict was suicide.

The law at San Pedro was represented by the comisario, his appointed assistants, and a *juez* (judge, corresponding to our justice of the peace). All were on the company payroll even though they were state officials. Casas Grandes, the head of the district, had a superior court, and a company of mounted federal police known as *Rurales*, special military police, under jurisdiction of President Díaz himself. Their duty was to curb any disturbance, keep the administration informed, and carry out decrees of the local or federal court. The captain of the Rurales, who had power over life and death, was the terror of bandits and guerilla bands everywhere. His followers dealt out justice that bad men understood.[7]

Two or three times a year, often unexpectedly, a company of fifteen to thirty Rurales would visit Minas de San Pedro, ostensibly for "recruits." Invariably, before going into camp, the captain would call the office and ask if we had any men "to spare," meaning men we wanted to get rid of. This was our main outlet for suspected or known trouble agitators. If we had any, a list was made giving the man's name and place where he worked. Immediately, a corporal with two or more privates were sent to the mine designated and, with the timekeeper, remained near the exit. As the men came from work their names were called by the timekeeper, and if a man's name appeared on the list, he was simply grabbed by the Rurales and "recruited" to fill a vacancy either among the Rurales or the regular army. Naturally, news that the Rurales were coming or were already in camp spread rapidly, but no one knew how many were present or who they were after. So long as they remained, the mines were short of labor.

One time when the main body of Rurales was leaving, a corporal and two soldiers were left behind to pick up a missing "recruit." The three were camped in the company corral. Toward evening the two privates returned from "old town," a Mexican village, feeling gay from too much mescal. One of them made a rash remark to the corporal, then — swish, whang; a sword slashed at a high-pointed sombrero, and the skull was cleft in twain. Seeing the crowd I went over to investigate. At sight of the body (not knowing any better), I inadvertently asked our chief of police why he did not arrest the corporal. "Sh-sh — Rurales," was all he said.

Next day, when the main group of about twenty returned, the captain came over to the office and with what I considered excess firmness and egotism, told me "where-to-get-off." He said words that implied that no state or local official, no foreigner or foreign government, had the power or authority to direct him or one of his men under any circumstances. Emphatically he stated: "Nobody, except *El Señor Presidente Don Porfirio Díaz!*" I did not understand all he said, but got the idea fully. Thenceforward, I let Mr. Díaz's Rurales run their own business. I remembered that Mr. Davis only a short time before had told me to "let their politics alone."

One payday two Americans, each with a roll of money visible in his shirt pocket, visited "old town." They took on a supply of liquor, had supper at a Mexican eating house, and started back to camp. Followed by three Mexicans, they resisted a hold-up and one of the Americans was killed.

We had just blown out the lamp and gone to bed when we heard a loud knocking at the door, and upon inquiry, recognized the voice of Forest Smith, an old-time friend of White Oaks days, who was then a level boss at one of the San Pedro mines. Unusually tall, well proportioned, good-looking with fair complexion, under the circumstances he was a weird and inglorious visitor because he was disheveled, bruised, pop-eyed, excited, and out of breath from running. He had a real case of scare-after-the-danger-is-passed, if you know what I mean. Following a brief explanation with the *Jefe de Político*, who lived next door, Smith and I walked back and found the American (whose name I have forgotten) lying stone dead. He was killed where he fell, and his roll of money was gone. Smith's description of the assailants was meager and uncertain. There were two young men, one apparently unarmed and the other holding a hunting knife; a third, older man, was past middle age and wore a wide brim high pointed hat and carried a six-shooter. He was the one who fired the fatal shot, the only one fired.

Notified by wire, the Rurales appeared the next day. Two days later one of the men was picked up hiding under a railway culvert

40 miles north. Protesting his own innocence, that he was unarmed and ran when the shot was fired, he confessed and provided a description of the others involved. The older man, who wore a large pointed sombrero and had the index finger missing from his right hand, was recognized as an itinerant peddler who had recently arrived in camp. Telegrams giving descriptions were sent in all directions. One, to the chief of police at Juárez, was delivered by messenger as he was walking through the plaza. He still held it in his hand when his attention focused on a broad-brim hat under which the face was hidden. At the chief's command, "Look up," the face appeared; at the order, "Hold up your hands," the chief saw that the telltale finger was missing.

Quick thinking, quick result! Returned to San Pedro, the man denied any connection with the crime. A couple of hundred pesos in his pocket was accounted for as the result of recent sales of knicknacks, and his presence in Juárez as a trip to replenish his stock. The trial was held in the San Pedro courtroom, the juez presiding. Half the morning and several hours of the afternoon were used in taking and writing down the testimony.

Naturally a crowd gathered on the patio outside. To use up spare time while waiting, a more interesting spectacle was staged — a cockfight, something in the title class of local sport. When the cocks were ready and the fight about to start, court was adjourned. The judge, the captain, the Rurales, and both prisoners left the courtroom to fraternize among the spectators, place their bets, and watch the fight. Court reconvened and the trial went on. As this was a federal case, the local judge made no decision, except to refer it to the higher court at Casas Grandes. The evidence, while circumstantial, favored a conviction.

Next day, the two prisoners walked as fifteen or twenty Rurales followed on horseback. The group was going toward Casas Grandes, but they stopped at Corralitos to stay the night. Early the next morning the march was resumed. In an open country with cattle grazing on either side, the prisoners abreast, they trudged along the dry, dusty road. When out about two miles at a prearranged signal from the captain, a chosen number of Rurales dismounted with loaded rifles in hand. A second signal, and one of the prisoners dropped with half a dozen bullets in his back. It was the elderly man, the man with the missing finger. The other stopped in his tracks, making no effort to run. The march was resumed with one prisoner now walking alone. A corporal and two Rurales returned to Corralitos to advise the authorities to go out to bring in and bury the corpse.

Hacienda Durazo,
Sonora

DURING THE SPRING OF 1901, the year before we left San Pedro, I made my first trip to Sonora, on the "other side" of the Sierra Madre range, to examine several mining properties near the towns of Moctezuma[1] and Lampazos.[2] These towns are about 175 miles below the border where the cities of Douglas, Arizona,[3] and Agua Prieta, Sonora,[4] now stand. The topography of west-central Mexico does not lend itself to east-west travel by road! Thousands of square miles of her territory are disrupted, torn, and gashed by high mountain ranges and deep valleys to such extent that costs of road construction have been and probably always will remain prohibitive. Other than trails, there are no connecting links between the plateau and the west coast except two semi-passable roadways, one near the United States border and the other, 1000 miles south, "The Barranca Passage" between Guadalajara and Tepic.[5]

Our conveyance for the first half of this 600-mile two-way journey was a buckboard with two mules. We rode in one of the first vehicles to pass over this uncharted northern route! The way was rough and tortuous as we ventured into the unknown. For long distances it was little more than a cattle trail between water holes and for miles we had no road at all, just a general direction. Companions on the trip were Tom Booz, superintendent of a mine near San Pedro, and Charlie Smith, a prospector who served as guide. Knowing that the end portion of the journey would necessarily be by horse or muleback, Smith rode my personal saddle horse, Prieta.

Westward from Minas de San Pedro to the Fronteras Valley[6] was by way of wide open spaces and winding passes among the foothills. The path passed three large ranches, the Corralitos, the Beresford, and the Boyd. The first two were stocked with white-face Herefords and the Boyd with black hornless Poll-Angus, each animal of its breed being sleek and fat and an exact duplicate of the others. It was a marvelous sight. From the Boyd ranch we journeyed down Pulpit Canyon, the rough, rocky "bottle-neck" between the two states of Chihuahua and Sonora, a drop by no means uniform of more than half a mile in about 5 miles. Ours was not the first wagon to negotiate this canyon, but certainly it was among the first half dozen, and probably it was the first to do so without the aid of block and tackle. Twice it was necessary to

Campsite of Parker and companion Tom Booz (center),
on one of the first trips by buckboard across the
Sierra Madre range from San Pedro to Moctezuma
and Lampazos, Sonora. To the right is Parker's
favorite saddle horse, Prieta.

Heading west from San Pedro across
Corralitos Flats. Parker snapped this photo
from his buckboard as
he passed a pack train loaded with ore
from distant mountains.

unhitch the mules and lower the buckboard by hand. To drive
up the gorge would have been impossible. The exit landed us
on the right (north) bank of the Big Bend of the Yaqui River,
whence, snakelike we continued westward to the Mormon settlement of Morelos.[7]

From near Morelos, across the river, could be seen plainly the
big earthquake crack, a straight, black streak, where in 1887 a
violent seismic disturbance had split the mountain along its western slope for miles. Two days later and 30 miles west at Fronteras,
we saw evidence of its destruction. Adobe houses were laid in
ruins with fallen roofs and walls which had crushed and killed
a number of people.

A short distance below Morelos we stopped alongside a group
of Mormon men and boys who were near the river fishing without line, hook, or bait. At that time of year the stream was low and
semi-clear and the water flowed gently. A half stick of dynamite

with a cap and short fuse was lighted and thrown to the center of a likely pool. A big splash accompanied the explosion, and then fish galore, dead fish, floated downstream. Naked young men and boys took over, swimming, diving, retrieving the kill. A dozen or more catfish weighing ten to twenty pounds each were thrown ashore, but the really big ones, stunned only by the explosion, lay at the bottom of the pool. They were prize objects of the divers and when found were buoyed to the surface and floated to the shore. Before leaving they gave us one about thirty inches long. The big one of the catch, a fifty pounder, was hung by the gills over the horn of a saddle, his tail reaching to the horse's knee. That scores of other fish were killed and floated downstream was a matter of exciting comment but otherwise of no consideration.

Incidentally, in this same vicinity some years later I learned how Mexicans catch catfish without powder. A homemade baited hook at one end of a long line is thrown into the stream, while the other end is tied to a bush on the bank which has a cowbell or tin can with loose pebbles inside fastened to the same branch. The fisherman patiently squats nearby or reclines sleeping on the sand. The ringing of the bell records a strike, and the louder the ring the bigger the fish.

To reach the Fronteras Valley from Morelos, it was necessary to trek northwest by ruts and gullies, avoiding brush and rocks, to within 15 or 20 miles of the United States border, then go west to a wagon road leading south to Moctezuma. This was the first real road we had traveled since leaving Corralitos. Moctezuma, locally and more familiarly known as Oposura, was an old pre-Spanish settlement 150 miles from the border. It was the county seat, the third or fourth largest town in Sonora, and the center of a rich agricultural and mining district. In spite of, or perhaps because of, occasional difficulties, the entire trip was an experience that enlivened the senses of outdoor enthusiasts. It was made up of crisp fresh air, vegetation, trees, shrubs, cacti, grass, wild flowers and birds, grazing cattle, an occasional band of sheep, covey of quail, rabbits, coyotes, foxes, deer, the ever changing scenery and mountain shadows on fantastic rock formations, gorgeous sunsets, and, at night, the big, bright stars and moon.

At Moctezuma, the end of the wagon road, when we were confronted with the impossibility of returning by the Pulpit Canyon route over which we had come, the buckboard and harness were sold. Thereafter the journey was continued with Booz and Charlie each mounted on one of the buckboard mules and myself on Prieta, my San Pedro saddle horse. Two pack mules and aparejos were purchased to carry our beds, baggage, and grub box. From there we traveled by trail, no longer apprehensive of a forced detour or bottleneck to delay our advance. We went on to Lampazos 25 miles to the south, then 12 miles west to El Gavilán,[8] our furthermost destination. There we found several old mine workings with ore exposed, and one larger dump at the entrance to a tunnel of El Carmen, the main workings on the property.

Arriving late, we ate supper and unrolled our bedding on a more or less level surface of the dump, and prepared for sleep, which under the circumstances was a welcome event. We did not sleep long. Confounded by the number of insects crawling over our faces, hands, and arms, we brushed off and smashed a few before we recognized the sweet-smelling dead animal odor and proceeded in haste to investigate. Lighting candles, we discovered that the place was swarming with, literally overrun by, thousands of granddaddy long-legs.[9] With no chance for survival at the place chosen for our night's rest, a hasty retreat was imperative with no time lost for argument! Gathering our beds we backtracked down the hill, until we found a place far enough removed and sufficiently level to make up the beds and spend the night. Before retiring, we carefully shook each piece of the bedding.

The next day on walking into the tunnel we noticed hanging to the walls and roof what at first appeared as a heavy fungus growth of granddaddy long-legs. With their bodies clustered close together and their long legs extended straight backwards, they formed solid mats in segregated patches ranging from a square foot to two square yards or more of covered surface. Stroking one of these mats was like stroking the mass of waving hair of a bear rug. Both the color and appearance in fact were quite similar to that of a brown bear. They reminded me somewhat of bats in limestone caves. A lighted candle thrust into the mass caused a singeing, burning streak as far as the flame extended and plenty of distinctive odor.

The property proved to be a large, low-grade deposit of lead carbonate and silver which had fair transportation facilities. It was a potential producer. There was talk of the Southern Pacific building a connecting line down the Moctezuma Valley which would materially increase activity and production of a number of mines in that region. As surveyed, the railroad would be only 9 miles distant from El Gavilán instead of the 185 miles to Bisbee, Arizona.[10]

From Lampazos, which was for many years one of the big silver producing camps of northern Mexico, we followed a well timbered trail north and east to the hacienda of Don Venancio Durazo[11] which was situated on the west bank of the Yaqui River. Don Venancio, as customary with such hacendadores, extended to us a kindly welcome and the hospitality of his home. On learning that we were interested in mines, he invited us to inspect a couple of workings from which he was then packing in ore for treatment in the patio of his hacienda. They proved to be little more than prospects, yet worthy of more development. Personally, I took an option on the El Carmen, for work to begin within sixty days but no payment to be made for six months. From there we started for home. Our journey west had required ten days by road, but the return trip from the hacienda took us four days by trail, and at no point were we within sight of our westbound route.

On reaching home at Minas de San Pedro, arrangements were made with Tom Davenport,[12] one of the mine foremen, to assume charge of the newly acquired mining prospect El Carmen. Within a few weeks we were on our way back across the mountains again

*El Carmen, near Lampazos, Sonora,
was the end of the trail —
reached by horseback —
for Parker and his companions.
The ore in this region
was too rich to mine.*

with two mozos and a pack train loaded with tools, a wheelbarrow, a portable assay outfit, dynamite and other supplies. Upon reaching camp, plans were made for future work and a credit account acquired for supplies and provisions. Tom remained at the mine while I, during the ensuing months, made several long rugged hard trips back and forth from San Pedro, or to and from Moctezuma. Traffic on the trail was slight, and while tales of holdups and bandits were common enough, good luck and knowledge of the Rurales fairly offset any realistic fear that someday, somewhere, something unpleasant might happen.

One day, on the trail from Moctezuma, alone and on horseback, high up on the divide directly west of the mine, I conceived the idea of a short cross-cut to camp. Darkness overtook me about the time the summit was reached. Tying the horse to a tree and sitting against another with my rifle alongside, I slept. As soon as daylight appeared, I got my bearings, then started towards camp. Hardly had the sun appeared when progress in the direction I had chosen was stopped by a long, vertical bluff, an escarpment around which it was necessary to make my way down.

Dismounting, I led the horse to the edge of the cliff and looked over, in search of a break or some place of descent. The bluff at this point was some fifty to seventy-five feet almost straight down. A movement on the ground below attracted my attention under the trees directly below where I was standing. Watching, I saw several spotted tigers,[13] some full grown, others mere kittens, gamboling, playing, having a fine time. Before leaving I counted thirteen of them. My first impulse was to shoot and get a tiger pelt, but I concluded there were entirely too many. I was hunting, true, but hunting for a way to get to camp! Turning back, I led the horse carefully and silently as possible, got into the saddle and rode away.

Another time, and at nearly the same place on the trail where I started on the "short cut," I met two horsemen going in the opposite direction, toward Moctezuma. As they approached I noticed one of them shift his six-shooter scabbard toward the front, which to me was a suspicious move. As they came nearer they separated as though to "split the trail," a cardinal breach of etiquette. Each evidently intended to pass on opposite sides, with me in the center between them. Quickly turning my horse, I fell to the ground, at the same time jerking my rifle from its scabbard. Then, covering both men, I ordered them to get together, pronto! Feigning surprise at my action, with assurances that I misunderstood their intention, they passed down the trail. Standing until they were out of sight, I mounted and rode for a short distance at ordinary pace. Then, putting spurs to the horse, I made all possible speed until reaching camp.

The next morning, Tom and I rode back to Moctezuma. He was an old-time cowboy and reading tracks to him was like reading a newspaper. Before reaching the place of my experience the evening before, he plainly pointed to tracks of two horses coming into the trail, and not two hundred yards beyond the place of the encounter, tracks of two horses leaving it. Following the latter, they proved to be the tracks coming into the trail; proof enough, we thought, that the men soon after passing, had back-tracked for the purpose of cutting me off further ahead on the trail. My hurry-up ride, no doubt, prevented a second, perhaps more serious encounter.

While in Moctezuma our story was told to the chief of police. He was greatly interested and wanted a more complete description of the men. Then he told us if ever again that happened on the trail elsewhere in Mexico, to shoot first and talk afterwards. In reply to my answer "Yes, and spend the rest of my life in some disagreeable jail," he said, "Nothing of the sort. I'll write out an authorization right now." He really meant it, too. Nevertheless, I declined with thanks.

Tom stayed on at El Carmen for several months. Then one day I received a wire from Moctezuma saying: "Ore too rich to mine — better come over." In anticipation of something *big*, I did! On arriving at the mine the reason for Tom's telegram was apparent. The ore mined during the past several days was piled on the patio and was all so-called "picture rock," which had native silver visible on almost every piece. The face of the drift, the walls and roof for several feet back, glistened in the frail light of the candles, forming a beautiful sight, a veritable miner's dream. Further development was warranted so we decided to go to Moctezuma to the mineral agent's office to "denounce" (locate) more ground, because the option we held was rather cramped for any extended operations.

Here enters the villain!

For many years the principal citizen "boss" of the district was an American who owned a large mercantile store, several ranches, and a number of mine prospects. From him we bought our El Carmen provisions and supplies. Like a medieval baron of the district, whenever he wanted anything from the state government at Hermosillo, he went over and "bought out" the city. Everyone knew when he was in town because brass bands paraded, banquets were held, and music, dancing and free liquor were everywhere. Invariably he got what he was after!

The day Tom and I went to Moctezuma to make our denouncement, our mule packer went along with eight or ten mules to bring back supplies for continuing the work. Immediately upon our arrival we went to the mineral agent's office, explained our mission, presented a map showing the ground we wished to denounce, then arranged with him that his secretary write the denouncement, with description of the property, in correct Spanish and proper legal form. On his desk we laid the filing fee of thirty-five pesos.

The secretary started to write. Tom and I sat in the office waiting to sign the papers. Meanwhile, the agent left us, going to another part of the house. Very soon afterward we saw his son, a boy about twelve years old, go through the entrance hall adjoining the room in which we were sitting and with a folded paper in his hand run across the patio and enter the merchant's store. A few minutes later the boy returned, running. Almost immediately the mineral agent entered the office (the secretary not yet having finished the denouncement), and waving a paper which we plainly recognized as the one the boy had just delivered to him, said, "Very sorry, gentlemen; very sorry, but I find it will be impossible to accept your denouncement. Here I find another covering the same ground, and as it precedes yours I am compelled by law to file it ahead of the one you are now writing."

Tom turned livid. He was a large man and I knew his strength and also something of his temper. Rising to his feet, he seized the back of his chair and for a moment it appeared that Mr. Agent was a "bashed goose." Springing between them I quieted Tom somewhat and we left. He was for cleaning up the town, mineral agent and merchant both. We went to our room and there, after getting control of our anger a bit, talked it over. The cards were stacked against us because we were in the merchant's territory and *he was the law*.

Having made our decision we walked over to the store. Standing back of the counter the merchant saw us enter and said something to one of the clerks who disappeared into an adjacent room, then returned a few moments later, while he himself hurried to one end of the counter where we knew he kept a six-shooter. His shifting eyes showed confusion and surprise. When I spoke and said, "None of that — no fight — we're through — simply stopped by to pay our bill," it was plainly an effort for him to control his agitation. Such a remark was entirely unexpected, contrary to rules.

While the bookkeeper was busy with the account, the merchant wanted to talk, "Sorry to hear about the misunderstanding — surely we can get together on some kind of compromise." Tom flashed back with some choice epithets that only an ex-Arizona mule-skinner knows how to explode. A tense situation was saved by the bookkeeper's bringing on the bill, and I, for one, was relieved when Tom followed me out the door. As we left, we passed the chief of police and one of his men, leaning against the wall just outside the door — the result, we surmised, of the clerk's disappearance as we went in.

We were not the only recipients of this practice of hijacking at Moctezuma. Only a short time before, another, bigger hold-up occurred when three Americans came to town for the purpose of filing a denouncement on a rich silver find a couple of miles north of El Tigre. Arriving by stage late in the afternoon after the mineral agent's office was closed, they made the mistake of talking, displaying specimens of ore 70 percent by weight pure silver, and telling the purpose of their visit. On presenting their application next morning they were informed, "Too late." The official record, and date, showed that a denouncement was made the previous day covering the same ground. The property became known as the Cinco de Mayo, and the owner, Colonel Francisco García,[14] was a close friend of the aforesaid merchant and a politi cal protégé of Mexico City. The mine, a large high-grade deposit in limestone, was a profitable producer for years and one of the big silver mines of northern Sonora.

Arrangements were made to leave the next morning immediately after writing a long letter to Don Venancio Durazo telling him what had occurred, and making a present to him of all the tools, camp outfit, assay outfit, everything left at the mine. The pack train brought from camp for supplies, we sent back empty. Señor Durazo worked El Carmen as long as he could do so without machinery, treating the ores in his arrastra at the hacienda. Later, it was sold to a group of Americans, who installed equipment and a small mill and added its holdings to other prospects in the vicinity.

Students of old Spanish and pre-Spanish civilization, culture, architecture and general living conditions would find in the *Hacienda de Durazo*[15] a duplication of conditions centuries old in Mexico. Sometime during the early eighteenth century the royal Viceroy at Mexico City affixed his signature to a grant of land "*about* 100 leagues east of the Pacific Ocean, in Sonora, bounded on the east and west by high mountain ranges, a valley, through the center of which a mighty river flowed." Two villages, Huásabas[16] and Granados,[17] located on the bank of the river several miles apart were included in the hacienda holdings. Their populations were 1500 and 2000, respectively. The villages, farms and inhabitants were strictly communal, a practice of all haciendas in Mexico, and a percentage of all production was the property of the hacendador. Situated as the Durazo property was, on the fringe of Yaqui territory, isolated, far inland and distant from other Spanish settlements, a place where escape from serfdom was comparatively easy, a firm, yet kindly character was required to maintain and develop its potential resources.

Such a character was Don Venancio, a man whose traits were inherited from his ancestors. He was an old world aristocrat of Spanish nobility, straight as a ramrod, six feet tall, having a long gray beard, three score years of age, yet active and forceful in

Don Venancio Durazo,
owner of a hacienda near the El Carmen Mine,
where Parker stayed briefly
while working the mine.

every movement. A near perfect specimen of a biblical patriarch as depicted by artists, he was Lord and Master of more than he could survey from the second story of his house, an advantage point daily used for that purpose. Nothing escaped his observation, for he could ride, walk, shoot, and look after his worldly affairs, all in the day's routine. He asked no odds of any man.

Situated a mile west of the river, on a knoll, an ideal spot in the valley, was the home — hacienda headquarters — an adobe structure in the usual form of a square. Above the entrance passageway to the enclosure was a single room, a second story, with flat mud roof. Access to this higher roof was by means of an out-side ladder made of round poles and wooden rungs. Every morn-ing, early, about sunrise, Don Venancio would climb this ladder at his outlook station and stand, clad in a long cape overcoat, or blanket tightly wrapped around his shoulders, his broad brim, pointed hat, a conspicuous object in silhouette. Alone, rigidly erect, almost without movement he stood like a statue, facing east, his gaze venturing up the valley toward Huásabas or down it toward Granados. For an hour or more he watched the laborers on their way to the fields to irrigate, to cultivate, or to gather the crops. He saw the cowboys headed toward the range, sheep starting out to graze, as well as cattle, goats, pigs, burros, mules, and horses. Whatever was taking place on both sides of the river, he saw from his high station, through the clear atmosphere for miles, as far as the eye could see. *All his!* With this mental picture in mind, he would descend, and breakfast in due time would be served.

As surmised, Don Venancio seldom traveled outside the con-fines of his own domain. With his wife and large family, the affairs of his household and estate occupied all of his time. His influence and wealth were so immense that he, himself, did not know or realize how great they were. The Indians and mestizos on his land were self-sufficient in their requirements. The hacienda was an independent, almost entirely self-sustaining monarchy. The laws of Mexico for Don Venancio were conformable to his own ideas of administration; they assisted, yet did not bother him at all.

Adjoining the main patio of the hacienda was a large square enclosure, inside of which was the sugar mill and a *beneficio* (treatment plant for ores containing gold and/or silver). Each of these was the same as that in use and practiced by the Spaniards for centuries past. The sugarcane was first roasted over a hot fire and then crushed in a low, circular vat by a heavy upright circular stone drawn by a mule attached to a cross arm extending outside the vat, thus causing the stone to rotate and squeeze the juice from the cane. Through openings near and around the bottom of the vat the juice flowed to "catch basins," whence it was ladled to copper kettles of twenty-five- to thirty-gallon capacity, and boiled to a heavy consistency. Then it was ladled to molds for use or for market. When cold the sugar was hard like a rock. This, the crude, brown, common sugar of Mexico, was known as *pinoche*.

The beneficio consisted of a similar grinding mechanism, except that instead of the grindstone, two heavy flat rocks were dragged by hand or burro around the vat, called an *arrastra*. The ore, first crushed by hand to half inch size, was gradually fed to the arrastra and was thus ground to about ordinary window screen size. Capacity for the beneficio was about one ton per day. As grinding proceeded, water was added in a steady stream, about four parts by weight to one of ore, which, by suspension and flow, carried the finely ground pulp to and through the discharge openings.

When free gold was the sole object of recovery, mercury was sprinkled inside the arrastra. Due to the heavier weight, the gold and mercury naturally sank to the bottom, where by contact and attrition the mercury absorbed the gold, forming an amalgam which sought and filled all the uneven, low spaces of the rock-

An arrastra, *an ore-grinding mechanism pulled by
burros and used to recover gold and silver.*

cement basin. The "clean-up," made at irregular periods depending on the richness of the ores, was usually about once a week. The entire contents of the arrastra were then "panned" by hand, fifteen to twenty pounds to the pan. The bottom was scraped and brushed, and all cracks were cleaned wherever amalgam was visible.

A short distance to one side of the hacienda was the cigarette factory, a large thatch-roofed adobe structure with all four sides open to the weather. Under this were two 40-foot-long tables with benches. In front of each pile a young Indian or mestizo maid was seated on the bench, rolling cigarettes. Any white cowboy I ever saw roll a cigarette, on viewing this sight, would certainly blush twice. First, with pleasure at the many black-eyed, healthy maidens, and second, at the speed each could show in rolling a cigarette. Light brown paper cut to size, and tobacco, dried and crushed by hand, were placed before each girl by a young man of corresponding age. A few older women and men supervised the work. Cigarettes crimped at both ends and tied in bundles of thirty-six each were then sold outside the hacienda to various stores in the villages and towns of Sonora, Chihuahua, and elsewhere in Mexico. A retail price of three centavos per package was charged the consumer, but I do not know Don Venancio's wholesale price.

With pipe in hand, I requested a trial smoke, which seemed to please Don Venancio. While I smoked, he instructed one of the girls to prepare for me a batch of "*real* pipe tobacco." This she did by sprinkling a few drops of anise and quite a liberal amount of cognac with the tobacco, mixing it thoroughly by sifting through her fingers, then spreading it on a clean cloth in the sunshine to dry. Tying the tobacco (about two pounds) in the cloth, she handed it to Don Venancio, who in turn gave it to me. Thus prepared, the native tobacco makes a very good pipe smoke. Several times, in later months, I sent back for more.

Down toward the river was the tannery where hides were cured and tanned in bark solutions, and nearby, the leather factory where all kinds of leather goods were made. In the field back of the hacienda was an orchard, with oranges, figs, avocados, and native fruits. Against the adobe wall was the largest growth of prickly pear cacti I ever saw. The pears, when ripe, are bright red, pear-shaped though smaller than our common pear, and spotted with numerous clusters of very fine, short, needlelike stickers. The fruit, after removal of the stickers, is delicious, except for the many seeds.

Evidently Don Venancio had never heard of nor seen a lemon until we brought some along in our provision box. He was greatly interested, more so after tasting a whiskey highball containing some of the juice. We endeavored to explain how they were grown from the seed or by grafting on orange trees, the same tree bearing both lemons and oranges. Immediately he began picking up all the seeds from the lemon we had cut and requested us to save him the seeds from any others we might use while there, his purpose being to graft and plant them to see if they would grow. We gave him several lemons, for which he thanked us with expressions fit for the gift of a gold watch or something really valuable.

One afternoon we witnessed the sale of some cattle at the hacienda — an important event. Whether the deal involved one or five hundred, the procedure was the same. They were a motley bunch, poorly bred, small, mostly horn, hooves, and bone — the typical Mexican mountain stock, wild as deer and harder to handle. Driving the herd to a convenient point outside the corral, one animal at a time was selected, cut out and chased into the corral where it was lassoed, thrown, and tied, ready for the brand. Payment was then made — fifteen pesos for each animal ($7.00 United States currency) — after which a red-hot iron was raked across the old brand, and a second red-hot iron burned the new owner's brand in a different place. With a sharp knife, the two ears were cut to correspond to the new owner's ear mark. The animal, released, was then driven outside the corral towards others similarly branded in a herd on the opposite side to that from which he had entered.

The newly branded cattle were then driven by the new owner and the cowboys of both parties to a point on the boundary of the hacienda, the object of the seller's men (traditionally a matter of courtesy and bon voyage), designed to prevent the branding of other cattle from the range. Such was the custom for generations past, evidence of the simple life without the entanglements of arithmetic.

Meals at the hacienda were serious affairs to me. The heavy, massive homemade table was about five feet wide by twelve feet in length. Separately, in small pottery dishes were the hand ground salt, black and red pepper, and sugar roughly broken from the original solid cake. Also, for anyone and all, were a couple of tablespoon-size, badly worn brass spoons, two or three knives, but no forks. Family and guests passed the spoons one to another for stirring sugar in the coffee, while each man at the table was usually equipped with his own personal pocket or hunting knife. Food, such as we Americans handle with a fork, was pushed by folded tortillas, one in each hand, and conveyed to the mouth. Bowls of thin stew or soup were lifted by one or both hands and downed without ceremony or etiquette. The food was simple but wholesome.

Don Venancio's mozo who brought on the food was forty-five to fifty years of age, a dwarf, not hunchback, four-feet to four-and-one-half-feet tall. He was stoutly built and well proportioned. He was a busy man though no evidence of hurry was manifest. Two or three times during the meal he would bring in a stack of tortillas, big, thin, wheat pancakes, eighteen to twenty inches in diameter, balanced on one hand and arm. When his arm was extended at full length, the tortillas scraped along the top of the table as he unloaded the stack.

It was not considered polite to ask for a second helping unless at the last "course" which was almost invariably frijoles. And, until one became adept in the push-and-load folded tortilla system, difficulty was experienced in their delivery to the proper place of consumption. Never shall I forget the disgusted look on the young daughter's face as she threw a brass tablespoon across the table in front of me, one who was sadly deficient in the epicurean art of eating. The clatter of brass on wood was somewhat startling. Her expression plainly said, "Use that, you poor ignorant Gringo, if you cannot otherwise eat like a man." And so, in gratitude, mixed more or less with humiliation, I did.

Arriving at the hacienda late in the afternoon after four days in the saddle from San Pedro and a hard day ahead, Tom and I were greeted with the usual hullabaloo of welcome. A new face among the family group was Don Francisco, the eldest son, returned from college in Mexico City. He was a tall, fine-looking lad of about twenty years, an exact chip off the old block. Hardly had we dismounted when Don Venancio led us into the main reception room, eager to display the gift his son brought, a gramophone[18] with many records. Surely the boy had brought every record the stores of Mexico City could furnish. The old gentleman was like a boy with first bicycle, smiling and prancing around. Don Venancio insisted that we listen to several records before going to our room. The gramophone of 1901 was not an elaborately ornamented music machine. Among the first of its kind on the market, it consisted of a square box (10″x10″x5″). The records were eight inches in diameter and were marked on one side only. A short, sharp steel needle had to be replaced and the mechanism wound up after each record was played.

Immediately after supper the music was continued. Evidently news of the wonderful mechanical musical instrument had been broadcast in the two villages nearby and it was not long before there was quite an audience. The salon was a room about 30 feet long by 15 feet wide. Near one end was a table on which the gramophone rested and around all four sides were chairs. Younger people sat on the floor, while the main crowd remained outside. The doors and windows were wide open so all could hear.

There was complete silence while the music was on, then, every half hour or so, two bottles, one of cognac and the other tequila, were passed around on a hand-carved wooden tray with half a dozen or more *hand-hammered solid silver drinking cups.* In reply to my inquiry, Don Venancio said the cups were "muy antigua," made right there on the hacienda by one of his workmen's ancestors.

Time dragged heavily for Tom and me. Repeatedly we offered excuses and tried to get away, but without success. Finally about three o'clock in the morning while the tray and silver cups were again in circulation, we slipped off to bed. The next day Don Venancio insisted on our staying over another night, for more music and a dance in our honor. It took all of our combined best Spanish to get his permission and consent to continue on our way. We had had enough music to last a long, long time. Seems like, after nearly half a century, I can still hear that gramophone scratch!

Mexican Towns and Mining Camps Visited by Parker

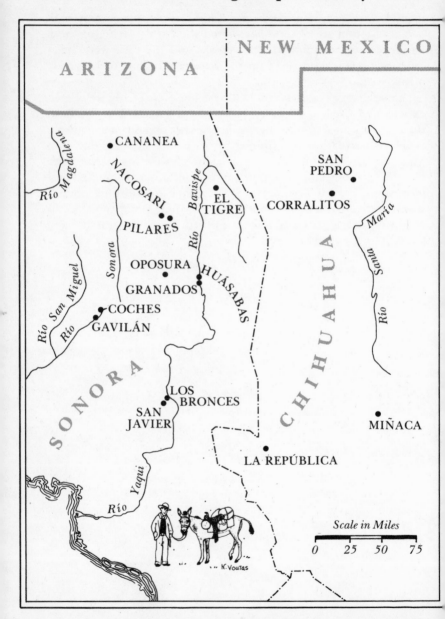

Pilares de Nacozari,
Sonora

AFTER LEAVING MINAS DE SAN PEDRO the family stayed for a short time in El Paso. Then we went back to the land of mañana to Pilares de Nacozari to work for the Moctezuma Copper Company, a subsidiary copper property of the Phelps Dodge Corporation managed by James S. Douglas, Jr.[1]

Mr. Douglas, familiarly known as "cuero crudo" to the Mexicans and "Rawhide Jimmy" to the Americans, was among the most colorful figures in Southwest mining history. He was highly respected, resourceful, and *a man of his word*. His father[2] for many years was president of the Phelps Dodge Corporation, and his son, Lewis,[3] in later years was appointed by President Franklin Roosevelt as Director of the Budget, and by President Harry Truman as United States Ambassador to England. Incidentally, to those of us who knew his father and grandfather, it was no surprise that Lewis so quickly resigned as budget director in the about-face of the New Deal Administration and its repudiation of the economy platform by which it came into power and under which Lewis had accepted the position.

The nickname "Rawhide" for James, Jr., originated at Prescott, Arizona, where he was engaged in mining before going to Nacozari. Of Scottish ancestry, by nature jovial as well as frugal, he thoroughly enjoyed a joke, more so when he, himself, might be the target. Apropos is the tale of a countryman who would stoop over a twenty-dollar gold piece to pick up a dime; in quick repartee

*Parker, with rifle, aboard
the stage from Douglas in 1901,
bound for Nacozari.*

he would argue, "Quite right, pick up the dime first, otherwise in all probability it would be ignored. Little things come first."

The following story was fresh when I arrived at Pilares. Construction on the narrow-gauge railway mine to the mill, from Nacozari to Pilares,[4] was within a day or two of being finished under the supervision of a jolly old-time mechanic named York, familiarly known as Tio (uncle). Mr. Douglas, walking along the ties and roadbed making final inspection, stopped to chat with Tio, who, with his men, was hard at work, his face, chest, and arms covered with perspiration. In his hand Mr. Douglas was carrying a bent railroad spike, one evidently thrown away. "Tio," he said, "this by itself doesn't amount to much, but a keg of them costs $4.50. It could, you know, be straightened and used."

The story I like best, and one more in line with his character, occurred shortly after I went to Pilares. Returning from New York, having gone there to assist in the sale of the Big Bug mine near Prescott, where he was manager before Pilares,[5] he told me of his trip, and in the course of the conversation said, "We made a good deal, sold out, lock, stock and barrel; price $200,000 cash and the balance on time. So far as I am concerned I don't care if we never get another dollar; we've already got all it is worth." A couple of months later he handed me a copy of the *Prescott Courier* newspaper, with big headlines across the front page, "Phenomenal Strike Big Bug Copper - 12 ft. Vein 14% Copper Ore." Smiling, not waiting for me to read the details, he said, "Now what do you think of *that?*" "Looks good," I replied, and then, "Looks to me like you might get your second payment." Quick, with both arms extended above his head (a well-known expressive gesture for Mr. Douglas) and an extra broad smile he bellowed: "Just exactly what I thought. And I hope they make a million dollars plus — more power to them." There was not a flicker to indicate the least regret or envy.

Nacozari is 80 miles south of the present-day border towns of Douglas, Arizona, and Agua Prieta, Sonora, both of which were surveyed and laid out in 1901. Pilares, the name derived from prominent "pillars," outcrops of blue-green stains of copper at the summit of the ridge, is literally and truly "a mine on the other side of the mountain."

Pilares Mine, Nacozari, Sonora, 1902. It grew
from a mill with 200-ton daily capacity to one of 3500 tons daily.

Previously, before acquisition by Phelps Dodge in 1900, the ore body was exploited by the American Smelting & Refining Company (A.S.&R.) and a smelter was built at Placeritos, 3 miles below Nacozari.[6] But, because of the nature of the ore, which was refractory, low-grade iron-copper sulphide, the impractical treatment and high costs, the venture was a failure. The deepest work was then less than 200 feet.

That Phelps Dodge might succeed where the A.S.&R. had failed required a lot of nerve, optimism, money — and management. At age thirty-five, James Douglas, Jr., already had a reputation: "Whenever they have a hard nut to crack, Phelps Dodge turns the job over to Jimmy," was a common camp expression. Pilares was no exception. The new plans embraced a complete change of approach, including the method of ore treatment, so Placeritos and all its equipment was abandoned. Concentration was to replace the smelting. The main and biggest problem was transportation.

Under the Phelps Dodge management of James Douglas, Jr., the new town and millsite selected were Nacozari, in the valley above Placeritos and 6 miles west of Pilares. From there a 36-inch-gauge railroad was built in two sections, one a 600-foot incline-tram. They were used to haul supplies to the mine and ore to the mill. The first mill, daily capacity 200 tons, and rail connections were completed a few days after I reached Pilares. From this meager beginning Pilares became one of the most productive and profitable mines of the entire Phelps Dodge holdings, worked to a depth of 2200 feet, with a daily mill capacity of 3500 tons.

At the time we went to Pilares, operations under Mr. Douglas had already been going on about two years. In the meantime, as a part of the corporation's expansion plans in New Mexico and Arizona, the El Paso and Southwestern Railroad,[7] now a part of the Southern Pacific, was under construction, having reached Douglas with work trains only. It was an unusual place to take my wife and three small children, the oldest not yet four-and-a-half years of age. By actual count it required fourteen transfers to

*The Pilares jib-back counterbalanced incline tramway.
Empty cars are pulled up the 600-foot incline by cars
loaded with ore. At lower left is the
Porvenir Tunnel which connects to the Pilares shaft.*

make the move from El Paso to Pilares. Furniture came first, then the family. We left El Paso in a secondhand day coach, going 100 miles to Hachita, New Mexico, about halfway to Douglas. Then we went from coach to a caboose attached to the end of a supply work train. From Douglas to Nacozari, 90 miles to the south, one and all piled into a three-seat stagecoach drawn by four horses. We stopped overnight at Cos, a halfway station, then returned again into our coach to drive on to Nacozari.

From there we walked, carrying the eight-month-old baby across the valley and bridge, then up the hill several hundred feet to the narrow-gauge railway leading to the mine. From there we rode 5.5 miles in an open 5-ton flat-bottom ore car at the tail end of a string of fifteen similar cars to a point on the west slope of Pilares mountain. Then, the big thrill! We went up the side of the mountain, an incline 1800 feet long (600 feet vertical elevation), to an upper, level track. There we were "unhitched" from the other cars and *our* car was hauled by three mules in tandem to the west base of the main Pilares ridge. We then walked 1500 feet through a tunnel to the opposite side of the ridge to the patio of the main shaft, where the office building, store, and warehouse were located. Outlined beyond the summit of a secondary ridge, were six frame buildings, three to five rooms each, for the Americans and selected Mexican employees. We were to occupy one of them.

The first thing we did was to build a yard and fence around the house. For a backyard, on account of the steep hillslope, a loose rock retaining wall was built several feet high and filled with stones and gravel. It made a nice backyard, one we were quite proud of and the children enjoyed until the first hard rain caused the filled-in portion — the whole backyard — to slide down the hill. The larger rocks went all the way to the canyon floor several hundred feet below. The next retaining wall was not so high, the yard not so large.

Assisting with the mine work, I had only five Americans. Among the miners were a number of Yaqui Indians who were

*The house where Parker lived with his family
while working the Pilares Mine,*
(second row, third from the right) .

quick to learn and, after a short period of training made excellent
miners, the best in Mexico. They were, as a rule, well built, active,
strong, not afraid of work, good natured and easy to get along
with. However, twice a year, early summer and fall, the time for
planting corn or wheat and the time for harvest, they simply
stopped work and went home. Anticipating this condition, it was
our policy to break all the ore possible, to hire every applicant for
work and to fill the various stopes (worked out areas), so that,
during their absence, the output, such as shoveling and bringing
to the surface the broken ore, could be maintained by the remaining Mexican laborers. Thus, there was no stoppage of production,
merely a temporary inconvenience.

During these periods of "migration," until a more stringent
method was devised for checking the drill steel used by the miners,
the supply suffered an abnormal shortage. In explanation, we
learned that planting corn involved pushing or driving a pointed
stick in the ground, dropping a few kernels of grain in the hole,

Many of the Pilares miners were Yaqui Indians,
who Parker claimed were the best miners in Mexico.
They are standing beside the ore bin and surface engine.

covering with soil, and tamping it slightly with the heel. Drill
steel, in lengths of 4 to 6 feet, made a superior prodding pole –
not only easier, but faster planting. Later developments showed
that Yaqui blacksmiths forged this steel into weapons of war,
knives, machetes, spear and arrow points, many of which were
among the weapons used by the Yaquis in their revolt against state
and federal troops a few years later.[8]

The ingenuity of the Yaqui is proverbial. To assist ventilation
underground, several hundred feet of 8- and 10-inch white canvas
hose was installed in various drifts and upraises through which
air from the compressor was forced to the workings. After a period
of "exodus," a goodly portion of the hose was missed. Also, the

store reported unusual sales of buttons, needles and strong white thread. In due course, when the Indians returned, we noticed them wearing white canvas trousers, stiff, uniform in circumference, baggy, and wearing quality to last a lifetime. The trousers themselves would have attracted a lot of attention without any knowledge of their origin. Another use had been discovered for the air hose! Visibly apparent, rough hewn top and bottom, no hems, the legs were unaltered, and the seat and waistband were made wider by simply sewing a V cut piece of canvas to the upper split seam of the air hose. The occasional lack of a button was remedied by the use of a sharp pointed tenpenny nail. Accused of pilfering, the only reply was a mischievous grin — *"Muy buenos pantalones, señor"* — the Yaquis considered their new trousers a big joke.

The 1500-foot tunnel through the mountain at Pilares was enlarged for a 36-inch-gauge track, and the 200-ton concentration plant at Nacozari was almost immediately enlarged to 1000 tons daily capacity. On this work, prior to production from the larger mill, approximately $1 million was spent. All the machinery, lumber, equipment and supplies were hauled by wagon from Don Luis, near Bisbee, Arizona, to Nacozari, a distance of 115 miles.

Heavy wagons and teams ranged to sixteen span, thirty-two horses or mules were used, and ten days to two weeks was good time for a round trip. With traffic in both directions, the long lines of wagons created sights and sounds which today are outmoded, and except as a record of history, forgotten, and impossible to imitate. During the rainy season long detours to and along the foothills of the Fronteras Valley were necessary. Even so, the wagons bogged axle deep in the black adobe soil, destroying the schedule completely.

Enlargement of the 1500-foot haulage tunnel at Pilares permitted extension of the 36-inch narrow-gauge track, mine to mill, which eliminated the necessity for the mule car through the tunnel and transfer to the 5-ton cars at the western portal. When completed, the big job then was to get a 15-ton Baldwin locomotive[9] up the 1800-foot incline connecting the lower and upper tracks. With anxious doubt and a couple of weeks preparation, during which the woodwork and frame of the drum brake at the upper station and a doubtful bridge about halfway up were strengthened, we overloaded the down platform and car. The holding brake was released and slowly the locomotive moved up the hill. Holding our breath and carefully watching each inch of upward progress, the feat was accomplished. Rolled from the tram platform onto the upper track rails, a bottle of champagne was broken over the cowcatcher, while the workmen subdued their bubble perspiration with a full case of cold beer.

Jesús García,[10] fireman of the lower track train since it began operating about six months earlier, was promoted to engineer of the upper train operating from the mine to the top station of the incline. He was a young man in his twenties, intelligent, level-headed, a good mechanic, dependable, proud of his engine and his work. About a year later the family and I left Pilares, and shortly thereafter García was again promoted. This time he was made chief engineer of the lower track and train. His services were satisfactory with no question or complaint.

A year or so later, he took a car loaded with 5 tons of dynamite from the magazine above the mill, and hooked it to the main string standing alongside the warehouse, where other cars were being loaded with merchandise and supplies for the mine. The routine of the day's work was broken by the dread cry of fire, *fire*. It was underneath, in the wood framework of the car containing the dynamite. How it started is unknown. Cordwood stacked alongside the track was not scorched. Perhaps a small trash pile, an oil soaked rag on the roadbed, a lighted match, cigarette, a spark from the engine caused the fire, but nobody knows. And, at the time nobody stood around to investigate and find out. At the sharp cry, "Fire!" now augmented by "Dynamite!" personal safety was the natural and uppermost thought of the crowd. Workmen loading supplies, passengers standing on the platform, families climbing on the ore cars for transportation to Pilares, and the daily mass of curious sightseers all stampeded for safety.

A moment only of futile effort existed as the blaze was growing bigger because no water was quickly available. Jesús García, with quick realization of the danger, jumped to his engine-cab, reversed the throttle, backed the lead cars a foot or two, stopped, jumped to the ground, ran back and uncoupled all cars behind the dynamite car, ran, leaped to the throttle and started full speed ahead. Not more than a quarter of a mile from the warehouse, the explosion occurred. Debris was scattered on the hillside, but nobody was hurt except the engineer, Jesús García.[11] He gave his life, made the supreme sacrifice, that others might live and the property of his employers not be destroyed. In memory, the name Nacozari was officially changed to *Nacozari de García*, by which the town has since been known. As a memorial, a replica of one of Europe's most famous fountains and statuary was carved and shipped from France or Italy, I have forgotten which, and placed in the main plaza of the town, where it now stands with his name and deed engraved thereon.

During this time and for years thereafter, power for all purposes was dependent on cordwood from the surrounding hills. Thus the countryside for 15 to 25 miles in all directions was entirely denuded of trees, and later along the railroad for 40 miles north as far as Cos, an equidistant on either side. Packed to the road by mules, hauled by wagons, this too required hundreds of animals.

Seventeen months at Pilares was enough! During this time, except for a few visits of American wives from Nacozari, there was no companionship for my wife except Mexican women. Fortunately, just before we left, Harry Melcher, the American store manager, was about to be married, and to him was sold all of our household possessions. Piling trunks and suitcases into an ore car, the family climbed on top and we went through the tunnel, down the incline, and traversed the narrow gauge with our car coupled at the tail end of some twenty-odd ore cars. Thus we managed our retreat.

On reaching level ground the children had a grand time running and playing without fear of stumbling or falling down the side of a mountain. Two days and nights were spent at the Douglas home, and a farewell dinner was given at the home of Mr. and Mrs. Williams,[12] the auditor and assistant manager. When we left Nacozari, a special coach was provided to carry the family to Cos, which at that time was the end of the railroad from Douglas. Then we boarded the train, had an overnight stop at Douglas, and finally arrived at El Paso, where henceforth we established a permanent home. The family no longer followed me around in and to mining camps with backyard playgrounds on mountain sides.

La República Mine, Chihuahua

THE STORY OF LA REPÚBLICA,[1] the big silver mine I bought on a *bluff*, centers about one of the most inaccessible mining regions of the Republic of Mexico. In far western Chihuahua, the mine was 110 miles from Miñaca, the nearest rail station, and six days hard travel on the back of a horse or mule on a rough mountain trail. Prior to any work being done, a one-half interest could have been purchased for $10,000. One year later the price, outright sale, option contract, was nearly a quarter of a million. Owners of the newly discovered prospect were three Americans: J. M. Gibbs and R. A. White, merchants at Miñaca, and Frank J. Alexander, president of one of the big insurance companies of the United States, who in this case was "out on his own."

Tales of tonnage and values enlarged each time either Gibbs or White visited El Paso and these aroused my curiosity, though doubts of their veracity remained uppermost in mind. The show-down came one evening at the Foreign Club of Chihuahua City, where I had gone to meet General Don Luis Terrazas to make final payment on a copper property known as El Rosario, owned by him and located about halfway between El Paso and Chihuahua, 20 miles west of the railroad.[2]

While waiting for papers to be drawn, several idle days gave White the opportunity of driving me to distraction. He was a good talker, a persistent character with a ready answer for every question. In desperation, to get rid of him, I played my trump

The original owner (center) of La República mining property with his family. They lived within view of a huge silver outcropping but only received a few hundred pesos for the house and land.

La República mining camp was six days hard travel by muleback over a rough mountain trail to the nearest rail station, Miñaca, 110 miles to the east.

card, the disconcerting squelcher, the "big bluff," frequently used before under similar circumstances and never called.

"All right," I said, "Get a piece of paper and write down what you have been telling me about the mine and values; then sign a check in my favor for $1000. I, in turn, will sign a sixty-day promissory note for $5000. An option contract will be drawn covering the price and terms of payment that you have outlined. Papers will be placed with Dale Brothers (an American bank in Chihuahua)[3] with a letter of instruction that, after examination and sampling by me, if any of the statements written by you are found incorrect, then your $1000 check is handed to me as expense money for the trip; on the other hand, if found correct, the $5000 note is yours, to apply as a first payment on the purchase price as mentioned in the option contract."

Instead of a deep groan or violent explosion such as I expected, after a few casual remarks to make the understanding clear, White rose from his chair, slapped me on the shoulder and with a broad smile said, "Parker, you've done something."

He was right, though at the time I did not realize its significance.

During the next day or two papers were signed and left at the bank. Then, having completed the Rosario deal, I returned to El Paso and explained to a few friends what I had done. I made arrangements for leaving other matters pending and within a couple of days was on my way to La República. From Chihuahua I was accompanied by Jim Murray, guide and agent of the owners, and another American, Dan Curley. With two pack animals and a mozo, we headed west from Miñaca.

Murray, with a superior mountain-bred horse and good American saddle, had just recently returned from the mine and therefore was physically hardened, while neither Curley nor myself had ridden a horse for several months — our flesh and muscles were soft. And how that man Murray could ride! With no regard for his fellow travelers, perhaps in an effort to show the distance was not as long as it really was, he prodded his own good steed and likewise our less able, swaybacked, worn-out and poorly equipped cayuses. At Tomochi,[4] a small Indian settlement 15 miles from Miñaca, six hours in the saddle, I was ready to call a halt for the day, but not so Murray, who insisted on a few miles more. That we were riding horses instead of mules increased the hardship because in their stumbling efforts to avoid loose, rolling stones, each misstep reacted like a whip post and gave another blow on our already overtaxed muscles.

The trail to La República crosses two narrow remnants of the ancient continental plateau; the first, Mesa Correo, was about halfway, and had an elevation of 8000 feet, and the second, Taloycte, 7200 feet, three hours by muleback from the mine. The intervening "basin" was a mass of jagged peaks and valleys, 2000 to 4000 feet up and down. Other than the extensive forests of pine which cover the two plateau divides, trees and other vegetation are semitropical. Scrub oak predominates, with scatterings of "wild cotton" which grows on trees 6 to 12 feet in height and has bolls the size of a lemon. White, like long staple cotton, it is used by the natives for mattresses and pillows. It rapidly and easily packs hard, but when placed outside and exposed to warm sunshine, it regains its fleecy form and softness. Known as Indian floss, it is probably the same as present-day commercial kapok. Grazing spots are plentiful, except close in where they are overrun and eaten off by the pack mules. Wild animal life is scarce owing to the prowess and large number of packers who use bows and arrows about as much as firearms.

Bird life, however, is particularly noticeable in the immense flocks of parakeets, small bright colored "parrots" flying overhead with a clack-quack chatter that completely drowns all attempts at conversation by mule-borne travelers, either following one another or riding side by side along the trail.

The first trip to La República was made in five days. Of the number I afterward made, only once was this record equaled, and then on the best saddle mule I could buy and for which I paid

Parker, third from the left, *with company on Mesa Correo, elevation 8000 feet, on the trail to La República. The mesa was one of two narrow remnants of the ancient continental plateau.*

200 pesos. Standard price for a mule was 50 to 75 pesos. That mule was a fast stepper, larger than the ordinary Mexican mule, and I rode astride a light McClellan saddle.

Examination of the mine disclosed no exaggeration in the story told by the owners: "a wide, strong vein on which, entirely in 100-ounce silver ore, a shaft had been sunk to a depth of 90 feet, and drift from the bottom 60 ft." Careful sampling on all four sides of the work showed consistent, average assay values of 98.5 ounces of silver and .25 ounce of gold per ton, a phenomenal, meritorious prospect. A company was organized among El Paso friends and larger scale work was started, including the installation of mine equipment and a ten stamp, 40-ton capacity mill.

Within a radius of 50 to 60 miles of La República, it is, I feel, no exaggeration to say there have been at least that number of producing mines in the million-dollar class and scores of lesser magnitude. Known and worked for gold and silver only, most of them were antiguas. The nearby Ocampo Mine[5] was said to have been in continuous operation for 200 years. During La República operations from 1906 to 1913 there were ten to twelve such "million dollar" producing properties along trails converging at Miñaca, and that many or more had long since been abandoned. Thus, it will be noted that we were not alone in this vast network of mountain peaks and valleys.

*Ocampo Mine, among the "million dollar"
gold and silver mines near La República,
had a misty and traditional history.*

*Watterson Gold Mill and camp,
one-half mile down creek from Ocampo.*

About halfway to La República were two important gold-silver mining camps, Concheño[6] and Pinos Altos,[7] the former then operating with installation of a 100-stamp mill and 300-horsepower Corliss compound engine. To one who knows the size and mechanism of an engine of that type the wonder of its emplacement at such an out-of-the-way place is startling. In fact, a jolting surprise is always in store for the tenderfoot on his arrival at one of these big far-flung installations. The size and weight of the equipment and machinery, all brought in sectionalized on the back of a mule or carried by barefoot natives — flywheels 30 feet or more in diameter, cast iron stamp mortars each weighing 5600 pounds, monstrous cylinders for engines and air compressors, drums and cables for mine hoists, boilers, smoke stacks — is always awesome. For example: a 1-inch steel hoist cable weighs 1.6 pounds per foot: 1000 feet weighs 1600 pounds. To avoid cutting and subsequent splicing, 1000 feet of cable, an awkward load, requires at least ten mules on the trail; ten separate coils of cable, spaced about 10 feet apart, one for each mule in tandem, and a man for each mule. Only an expert mule packer can handle a cable and deliver it in anywhere near workable condition.

Fortunately, by building our own line to Sahuayacan,[8] a gold camp 10 miles south, La República was connected with the outside world by telephone, an item of an immense benefit to the company and a welcome adjunct to the military.

Exactly on the same date one year after I first saw La República, the mill started production, an accomplishment that was a record achievement in that district. The mill was a standard concentration-leaching (cyanide) plant with a capacity of 40 tons per 24 hours, and recovery of minerals was above 90 percent, half concentrates and half bullion. The concentrates approximated 2 tons per day since 20 tons of ore were required to make 1 ton of concentrates. The concentrates were shipped in 100-pound burlap sacks, with two sacks to each mule. The cyanide product amounted to two bars daily which weighed 100 pounds each. Gross production was $75,000 to $90,000 per month.

Provisions, supplies and all small articles were packed in strong burlap sacks, reinforced boxes and crates; pipe rods, and corrugated iron were dragged with one end on the ground. The more cumbersome and heavier machinery was cut and sectionalized to a maximum of 300 pounds for the mountain trail and muleback transportation. Where this was impossible, such as a #7 Cameron mine-sinking pump which weighed 450 pounds, the item was packed on an extra large, strong mule with two men to help over the rougher places. Three solid steel stamp mill cam shafts, 9 feet in length and weighing 700 pounds each, presented different problems. To transport the cam shafts, Pascual Orozco,[9] our head mule-freight contractor but afterwards *generalísimo* during the Madero revolution, was paid 700 pesos for each. Instead of mules, native Indians served as packers. Garbed with a G-string and a hat, wearing *huaraches* (sandals) or going barefoot, carrying a single blanket, a few pounds of ground corn and a little pinoche (crude cane sugar), the Indians were quite effective. To carry the load, two poles (each about 20 feet long) were lashed alongside a shaft, with cross pieces each 4 feet long, 2.5 to 3 feet apart. With eight men on a side, sixteen to each piece of shafting, the cargo was delivered from Miñaca to the mine in fourteen days, a feat that equaled the general mule train schedule. At every village along the trail, friends joined the procession to help or simply to encourage the packers and be with the crowd.

Incidentally, on the trail one day while headed toward Miñaca, I met one of the regular pack trains, one mule of which was bringing in the Cameron pump. The hind man, "pusher," was Pancho Villa,[10] chief assistant to Orozco. Villa later became a generalísimo, rebel chief, and superbandit. The man ahead was pulling on two ropes, one of which was attached to the pump and the other to the halter on the mule's head. Pancho Villa was behind, pushing, lifting, struggling, sweating up a steep, slippery hill in a drizzling rain. Stopping for a moment as I passed, in reply to my suggestion "Why not get out of the rain, why not mañana," he replied, "No, Señor Jefe (boss), this is my job. The pump will be there on the day I promised."

For La República, approximately 500 mules and a minimum of 75 men were on the trail daily, the former ironshod and the latter barefooted or wearing sandals. After about three round trips, a complete change of mules was necessary for rest, nourishment, and recovery from sore backs, cuts, and bruises. In addition to the above, 200 mules were engaged bringing in cordwood for use in the boilers at the mine and mill. Thus, since an equal number were on pasture, the operation required 1200 to 1500 mules. The market value of mules was 50 to 75 pesos, while *aparejos* (pack-saddles) cost 15 to 25 pesos.

Under normal conditions the ten to twelve "local" properties then operating in this region also required thousands of mules because of the supplies being carried in and the concentrates and bullion being taken out. When we consider that La República was but one of hundreds of mines, large and small throughout

Approximately 1500 mules such as these hauling lumber and packing supplies were necessary for efficient operation of La República Mine.

the mountain regions of Mexico, the number and importance of this small 700- to 800-pound animal is surprisingly significant and certainly a vitally necessary part of operations.

The usual "pack train" consisted of fifteen mules, with two to three *arrieros* (muleteers). With good weather, and uniform average weight and size of pack, the one-way trip of 110 miles was made to La República in twelve to fifteen days. As no grain or fodder was carried, the mules foraged for themselves. A day's journey involved an early morning start and five to eight hours continuous travel, with recurring halts to readjust unbalanced and shifting loads. After the selection of a camping place, where aparejos and cargas were removed, the animals were turned loose to graze. To protect sensitive freight such as sugar, beans, and coffee from rain, snow, or contact with brush, limbs of trees and high jagged rocks, the carga was covered by sheets of heavy canvas, furnished as a rule by the owner of the carga. The minimum base rate for a one-way carga was 9 pesos, equivalent to 60 pesos per ton ($30.00 United States currency), assuming that each carga weighed 300 pounds, an assumption that was the exception rather than the rule.

La República lay in a valley west of Tayolote mesa. From the edge of the mesa the trail descended along a thickly wooded ridge to a point north of and above the mine camp, whence, by a repetition of zigzags it descended to the floor of the valley and the camp. We did more work on this zigzag than all the rest of the trail from Miñaca. Horizontally and vertically the distance was about the same, 1800 feet, but on the back of a mule, or walking, it required a good three quarters of an hour's travel.

For our first dwellings, the warehouse and store, we resorted to the common practice of whipsawing lumber by hand. On the mesa where trees were felled, a platform was rigged 6 to 8 feet above the ground, onto which the log was rolled. With a two-handled whipsaw, one man on the platform, another below on the ground, the log was sawed lengthwise into whatever size was specified. Marked on the top with a string and chalk, it was surprising how accurately the men cut to the dimension line. The result was uniform-sized material. Lumber thus cut was dragged by mules down the trail to camp, one end tied to the *aparejo* and the other dragging behind.

A couple of hundred yards before the high point of the zigzag was reached, the trail passed over and above a vertical bluff, a drop of several hundred feet. The air space afforded by this bluff helped to solve the problem of getting logs from the mesa to the sawmill, which was erected in camp near the proposed mill site. Dragged to a prepared point, the logs were slid to the edge and pushed off, a stirring sight and sound to see them fall and hear the crash, like giants on a springboard, some making a perfect dive and some a bellybuster. When the mill was operating, those broken were used as cordwood.

Having solved the log problem, next on the list was to "un-water" the mine *without* a pump. Gravity, our ally in logging, was now the antagonist which threatened to stop all mine development. Fortunately, prior to the arrival and installation of the first boiler and steam pump, we had on hand a two-man hand-force pump which worked in a manner similar to a section tool-car on the railroad. This was installed on the 90-foot station, and the shaft was allowed to fill to this point. Then a suction hose was run into the water and a 1.5-inch iron discharge pipe was run to the surface. Three men were put on each eight-hour shift, one resting while the others pumped. Even so, nearly each shift required a new crew.

Something had to be done, or else close down the mine work. Then came an idea. One hundred yards upstream from the shaft the creek cut diagonally across the vein, then continued west along the hanging wall. The shaft was in the vein and about 15 feet above the creek, the collar (top) 12 to 15 feet lower in elevation than the point where the creek crossed. To one side of the stream in a depressed area near the crossing there was an appreciable spring of warm water where an excavation had been made and utilized by the workmen for bathing. Now, the water from the drift below was also lukewarm, indicating the same source as that of the surface spring. Near the end of the drift, 90 feet below the surface and 75 feet from the shaft, a concrete bulkhead was built, and a 2-inch pipe with valve outside the bulkhead was placed at the bottom. A discharge pipe was put along the floor of the drift and up the shaft and, presto, there was an artesian flow!

Incidentally, by placing an elbow and short piece of pipe and a platform below the new discharge, we had a warm shower bath at any time of day or night! It served its purpose, however, for now work could be resumed. Later on, depth and extension of levels greatly increased the flow of water in the mine, and pumping and timbering, next to labor, became the high costs of mining.

Excellent artisans among the Mexicans are not uncommon, a trait possibly of long heritage. They learned the hard way, by apprenticeship and copy, and often the secret of a family is handed down from father to son. Our Mexican blacksmith at La República was good, his steel and picks for the mine work being as near perfect as any I have ever known, and well tempered, and well shaped. I still have among my prized possessions, after nearly 40 years, the small prospector's pick he made for me from a ⅞-inch hexagon bar of drill steel. Brazed into the steel on one side is "M.B. Parker" and on the other "El Paso Texas." A perfectly cut "eye" for the handle, perfect balance, it has outlasted half a dozen or more store-picks purchased on trips when my usual kit had been left at home. That pick has been used by me from the southernmost parts of Mexico to Alaska.

During construction we had as millwright an excellent mechanic, an American from El Paso whose wages were $350.00 a month, a high figure for 1907. By comparison, our Mexican blacksmith, who was used for the mine work such as sharpening steel and picks, learned his trade as helper in other mine camps of the Rayón and Ocampo districts. His wages were 4.5 pesos ($2.25 United States currency) per day. Shortly after the mill started, a coil-spiral spring on one of the self-feeders in back of the batteries broke. From the warehouse stock of drawn steel bars the American mechanic made two springs, each of which lasted about half an hour. Taking the broken pieces of the original to our Mexican blacksmith, I asked him if he could make one. He hesitatingly replied that he would try.

With his helper he hammered a piece of ordinary drill steel, ⅞-inch hexagon, to a smaller diameter. Then with a swage, he hammered it to approximately the right size, ¼-inch diameter and 2 feet long. The original spring was about 1 inch inside diameter and 4 inches long. Clamping a short piece of 1-inch pipe in his bench vise, he heated the rod and made the spiral by winding it around the pipe. Now, it is well known that fish oil is an excellent medium for tempering tool steel. How he knew, or ever heard of it I do not know, but he asked for it and fortunately we had some in stock; with it he tempered the spring. What he handed me was not much for looks, but it did work. The American, when he saw it was perplexed at first, but then he made inquiries. When I told him the story, he good naturedly remarked, "That Mexican, by *hammering* the drill steel made *forged* steel, the stuff that springs are made of. My hat's off to him!" The above accomplishment (resourcefulness) saved the company the wages of nine pumpmen daily for at least a month, possibly two, because it was not necessary to send out for a new coil spring.

Of all the examples of inherent virtue among the mountain Indians of Mexico, unexcelled by modern civilization, none is more outstanding than the employment at La República of two young men to bring the payroll and expense money from Miñaca to the mine. The amount approximated 30,000 pesos ($15,000) per month. To get this from the railroad, two young Indians were employed at standard wages of $35.00 United States currency a month each. At intervals of about two weeks, one or the other, alone and afoot, would drop into Miñaca and there receive from our agent a small rectangular package containing so many 20s, 10s, 5s and 1 peso bills, and a canvas bag containing 100 pesos in silver and copper coins (small change) for delivery at the mine.

Their mark "X" on a standard printed form was our only evidence of receipt; neither of them could read or write. Each knew what he was carrying as well as the hazards of his mission; yet, they did their job.

The hillslope back of camp which possessed the long zigzag trail was but sparsely wooded, hence from there one had a clear view from camp almost to the summit. One day curiosity caused me to get out the binoculars for a closer view of some peculiar objects coming down the trail. What I saw was eleven men, each with a bulky package on his back, so large in fact that the load was almost as big as the man himself. I was unable to make out the strange procession and the binoculars were of little help as I awaited their arrival half an hour later. All were mountain Indians. Each of the men had on his back a full-size, complete Singer Sewing Machine which they had packed from Guerrero, a town 10 miles north of Miñaca.

They were followed a couple of hours later by a Mexican salesman and several mules with large crates containing clothing, suits and dresses, shoes, hats, and underwear. The sewing machines were a part of his stock. Part owner of a mercantile store at Guerrero, the enterprising young fellow told me this was a regular procedure with him for selling merchandise. On numerous trips to the various villages in the mountain region west of Guerrero failure to sell his entire stock was unknown, and new mining camps were sure things. That was his reason for no stops this trip along the way, except, he said, at one place where he was persuaded to sell one of the machines; hence the eleven delivered at La República.

Selling price of the sewing machines was 165 pesos ($82.50 United States currency); terms, 15 pesos down, and 10 pesos a month thereafter. An arrangement was made with the company's store clerk for collection. He told me that seldom, practically never, had he lost money in dealing with these mountain people. His prediction was verified since in an incredibly short time his entire stock was sold at La República. And that is not all. Some two months later when he returned, the man-borne cargo this time consisted of one dozen home range kitchen stoves; and they too were carried in by Indians, walking. The itinerant Yankee peddler would be a big laugh to a salesman of this type!

A puzzle-picture remains of what became of the sewing machines and cook stoves. Dwellings, mostly shacks, jacales for mine and camp employees are built by the laborers themselves, with little or no assistance from the management. They were small, mostly one room adobe or thatched-and-pole structures with mud roofs, and they invariably had dirt floors. An excavation is made on the hillside to create an open space, any place large enough to build on. A favored feature is the overhanging shed roof, with one wall of the house extended, thus making a somewhat protected corner for the outdoor fireplace, which was open to the elements, dust and rain. A wooden bedstead, a table, a bench make up the list of furniture. The majority of the family, usually large, sleeps on woven grass mats on the floor, inside or outside the house.

The jacales are always dark because wood shutters cover the window openings since there is no glass available. As a result, all sewing and other work is done outside. A number of the purchasers never before owned, probably never saw a sewing machine or stove. Yet, articles such as these, with a little money and a lot of credit, were eagerly pounced upon and highly prized as emblems of superiority and riches. As hospitality and share-with-others are also characteristics of all Indians, the machines soon became the gossip center of local "society," and were used by the owners, their friends and all the neighborhood. How long they ran or were kept in repair, I do not know. Often, when worn out and useless, they were stored inside the house as souvenirs.

Ice cream in Ocampo? No mechanical refrigeration, no pond for natural ice; how? Situated in a deep canyon, backed by cliffs rising 2000 feet and more with the sun shining straight down, the summer days are plenty hot. Precipitation from clouds high up in colder strata results in frequent hailstorms in the valley — hail like hen's eggs! Near the center of town, at the end of a short side street was an old abandoned mine tunnel. An ingenious Mexican merchant had his building close against the mountain with the back door being but a few steps from the tunnel entrance. This was the *icebox* of Ocampo!

Ice was supplied by hail and the townspeople in what was an amusing spectacle. Following a storm the streets and by-ways were filled with men, women, and children scampering, running, gathering hail to deliver to the store and tunnel, where each one's burden was weighed and credit given for future purchases. At times, in winter, to augment the supply, snow from the nearby higher slopes would be brought down by pack mules and added to the pile in the tunnel.

Evidently this was a paying business; the storekeeper kept ice, whereon was preserved beer, eggs, watermelon, vegetables, canned butter — and ice cream — the standard surprise and treat for Americans on their arrival at Ocampo.

I was caught on the trail one day near La República in one of those hailstorms and the experience was not pleasant. A double-thick, yellow cowboy slicker offered little protection. The old adage, "Never take shelter under a tree during a thunderstorm," may be good advice elsewhere, but not during a hailstorm in that country. Lightning may be quicker, but it certainly cannot hurt like hail.

The trail west from Ocampo to Moris[11] was the worst of any on our way to La República because we had a steep climb to the ridge before taking a long, rough grade down to the valley. On the way down there was a shortcut (not for animals with cargo), a narrow, one-way trail known as "The Cuchillo" (knife), because at a point circling the cliff was a scissor-turn so sharp that the mule's head projected over the south edge, his tail over the north — a sheer drop on three sides. Places like this are where a mule shows his superior intelligence over a horse. The experienced rider will sit tight and give the mule his own choice of speed and places to step. If dizzy or scared, you have to shut your eyes!

Our arrival at the settlement in the valley, also Cuchillo by name, was heralded by people running, not toward us, but to the opposite side of town. The story developed later: three men were hunting deer, two with .44 caliber Winchester rifles and the other unarmed. During an unexpected and sudden encounter with a full grown grizzly bear, the unarmed man started to run as the bear took after him. It takes a lot of lead to stop an enraged grizzly. I saw the pelt, and it was riddled with half a dozen or more bullet holes. The people we saw running were interested not in us, but in those carrying home the body of their fellow townsman, who had been torn to shreds by the bear.

In the churchyard at Cuchillo was a fresh grave and marker where lay the body of a priest who, only a few days before, on the shortcut Cuchillo trail at the scissor point, attempted to dismount, thus throwing his mule off balance. The mangled bodies of both man and mule were found among the rocks at the foot of the cliff, several hundred feet below the trail. Once was enough for me over that shortcut!

An instance of grief in efforts to improve transportation in the mountain sections of Mexico involved the Greene Gold-Silver Mining Company,[12] operating mines at Ocampo and other camps nearby. From Temósachic, a town some 40 miles northwest of Miñaca, they built a wagon road to Ocampo, 75 to 80 miles to the southwest. For the first 60 miles along the fairly uniform plateau, construction was normal, but from there on were continuous grading, cuts in solid rock, and bridges to erect. It was all hard work and cost about $350,000. Most of the cost was for the last few miles where the road dropped from the plateau with an elevation of 8000 feet to the village of Ocampo 4500 feet below. Included were long stretches of tunnel work with solid roof overhead, and short tunnels through projecting points cut into the perpendicular bluff. The resulting road was a suspended scratch line with horizontal trenches along the bluff. On the outer edge was a vertical drop of several hundred feet, so the road was plainly in view from Ocampo.

All necessary equipment for large-scale hauling had to be brought in, such as heavy freight wagons and big American mules. Change stations had to be built and supplied with hay and grain, and blacksmith shops had to be constructed. Finished, it was a fine example of engineering skill, a wonder-job well done.

It was a great day for the neighborhood when the road was opened formally. Mr. Greene, on a special train with stockholders from New York, state officials from Chihuahua City, friends from California, Arizona, and New Mexico, arrived with much fanfare at Temósachic. From there, with four large, new automobiles brought along on the train, the "journey of the nabobs" was conducted to Ocampo.[13] Never before had the old town known such festivities, especially since a large portion of its citizens had never seen an automobile before. Crowds came from settlements far back in the mountains, miles away. The road represented a means of transportation they had never even dreamed of before! Then, a couple of weeks later, one of those torrential thunderstorms with cloudburst attachments occurred, and in about an hour the Concheño-Ocampo portion of the road was back where it was before the third of a million dollars was spent; it was non-existent.

Before going further, a word should be included about Mr. William C. Greene. He was a typical westerner, a cowboy and prospector in early youth, a good spender whose affluence in later years did not cause him to forget nor neglect the friends of his own hard "digging" days. Reminiscent of this, in Juárez one morning, at the station to take the train to Casas Grandes, I met Mr. Greene who invited me to ride in his private car. With several of his New York associates we had a pleasant journey. At Guzmán, a station about halfway, the train stopped and we got off for a stroll along the platform.

Presently we saw among the second-class passengers a man we both knew, Charlie Smith, the prospector who rode my horse Prieta, when Tom Booz and I made our first trip from Minas de San Pedro over into Sonora. We all shook hands in friendly greeting. In reply to our questions, Smith told us he had been prospecting out beyond Casas Grandes and was on his way back. Greene asked, "How are you fixed for money, Charlie?" "Oh, all right," Charlie said. "Had a little hard luck last time, lost one of my mules, but I'm all right now." Fumbling in his left vest pocket, Greene pulled out several new, folded bills, calmly pulled off one and handed it to Smith. "Here, maybe this will help," he said. "When that's gone, let me know." It was a $500 bill, United States money. Flabbergasted, Smith endeavored to protest, but to no avail. "O.K. now Charlie. We're partners. Write to me and keep me posted. If you find anything worthwhile, maybe I can help you swing it." When the train started, Greene insisted that Charlie, overalls, battered hat, worn-out shoes, come along and ride in the private car with us.[14]

The discoverer and promoter of the vast copper deposits at Cananea, Sonora, Mr. Greene, after selling his holdings there, allowed himself to be persuaded by New York stockbrokers that millions could be raised for any mine enterprise with which his name might be connected. Concessions for prospecting and mining rights were secured on immense tracts in Sonora and Chihuahua, and a vast campaign of exploitation was undertaken. Among the early purchases was our old Minas de San Pedro railroad, the Río Grande, Sierra Madre and Pacific, which ran from Juárez to Terrazas. This was extended south by Mr. Green to connect with the Stilwell Kansas City, Mexico and Orient railroad west of Chihuahua City, at a point near Miñaca, and the third of a million dollar wagon road to Ocampo was built.[15] Also purchased were large timber tracts and several of the larger producing mines at Ocampo, Pinos Altos, Concheño, Boluda, El Trigo, Mulatos, and elsewhere.

When the New York sales of stock failed to produce sufficient funds, Mr. Greene threw his entire fortune of several millions into his ventures — and failed. Fortunately, before organizing the Greene Gold-Silver Company, he had transferred his large ranch near Cananea to his wife, so the ranch could not be taken by his creditors.

Later, at his home town of Cananea, he drove a span of beautiful, matched horses. As he was getting into the buggy one day, the horses started to run and he was thrown violently against the hitching post, his skull fractured. By his death the Southwest lost one of its most colorful figures.

For a year or so after the flood, freight from Temósachic to Concheño, a distance of 65 miles, was continued by means of the heavy wagons and big American mules, but those big mules had to be fed because self-grazing was impractical. It soon became evident that standard size and weight cargo could be delivered cheaper by pack mule than by wagon. The big mules were discarded, and lighter wagons and the small Mexican mules were substituted. The pack mule and arriero were back on the job to stay. The road was kept open, however, from Temósachic, but it was used only as far as Concheño, primarily for heavy machinery and for other material not readily transferable by aparejos and mules. And this by no means was the only road of its kind built and not used for long in the mining regions of the Sierra Madre.

The difficulty of getting pack mules headed the list for breakdowns in operations. Early in the Revolution, which began in 1910, our bullion conductor, Juan Chávez,[16] joined the insurgent forces as a generalísimo and was killed in one of the first skirmishes, not far from Miñaca. Guerrillas soon took over the mountain region, but despite the forays, work continued for several months. When the trail to Miñaca became "too hot," a new trail was opened to the south and west to El Fuerte, the terminal of the Kansas City, Mexico and Orient (Stilwell Railway). Not only were the pack trains held up, the cargo looted, and mules confiscated, but, as the bandits grew bolder, settlements and mining camps were entered, stores and warehouses were stripped, and materials and supplies were carried away or destroyed. Three times La República was a victim. It was practically cleaned out as the goods were paid for by worthless IOUs. The bullion pack trains became a prize objective, as well they might, for each mule carried $2,000 in silver on his back. Often a train carried 20,000 pesos at the wild exchange rates then prevailing.

As time went on, conditions grew worse. Independent bands of bandits, parading as government troops, became more numerous and bold. Skirmishes occurred, men were killed or wounded and supplies and bullion were lost. The final knockout came when, soon after a bullion train left camp, bandits entered and practically cleaned out both the store and warehouse. Next day the bullion train on the trail was overtaken and attacked, and the conductor (an American) and one of his men were killed. Others were wounded and the bullion was lost and scattered. To the credit of local officials, a considerable portion of the bullion was subsequently recovered. So heavy a weight in such a small package is hard to conceal, and since a bar of silver bullion contains the name or initial of its owner, it is easily identified and thus hard to dispose of. Some, unquestionably, was buried for future removal and may never be found.

La República was closed down in 1912–13. A caretaker was left to look after the camp, and the holding tax was paid for several years. Because of the existing chaos and continued revolutions, it became obvious that there was no possibility of renewing operations so the property was abandoned. Mexican mining laws under the Díaz regime were liberal, as a holding tax of about $1.00 per acre assured possession. No taxes were levied on evaluation or improvements, only on *production*, which before the revolution was about seven percent on silver. Failure to pay the holding tax resulted in loss of title, with the property reverting to the government. Further action was subject to relocation which included all unclaimed surface equipment and improvements.

Local Mexicans took possession of La República, but with buildings dismantled, machinery ruined, and the mine flooded, no efforts so far as I know have since been attempted to renew operations. Although unquestionably good ore still remains, and probably a lot of it, the costs of rehabilitation are beyond the reach of any small operator, and a large operator would be skeptical and not inclined to risk the sum involved. Like many other mines in Mexico, La República is but an example of the effect the revolution had on mining as well as on other industries.

The Revolution:
Trails, Muleteers and
Generalísimos

BECAUSE OF THE LONGTIME WEAR and number of passing and repassing pack trains the trails are often as wide as city streets, yet they are never cleared of rocks and pebbles. The result is a continuous corrugated surface, alternating in smooth stepping spaces and ridges of loose stones, spaced by the footsteps of the mules to fit their stepping distance. For this reason the experienced traveler selects and prefers to ride a mule. A horse takes a longer stride, hence by constant sliding and slipping on the rolling stones he soon becomes lame and the rider is shaken and sore.

An interesting and sometimes very aggravating variation occurs where the trail passes over formations of soft sandstone or solidified volcanic ash. Here the trail becomes a mass of channels or ditches, parallel, criss-crossing and separated by ridges, and worn to such a depth that a rider's stirrup will scrape each side, compelling him to raise both legs. A sharp lookout is necessary in order to select and follow a trench not too deep for passing, or, possibly for exit. Two loaded pack trains meeting in such a place may mean a lot of grief, with unloading one of the mules as the only obvious answer.

In formations of this nature the trail markings are not only much wider than ordinary, but wide detours are often necessary as the channels, once started, are rapidly cut deeper by both mulewear and erosion. Approaches to many of the villages throughout Mexico show this trenching to a remarkable degree, some of which is centuries old. Personal muleback travel from Miñaca to La

República mine required six to seven days of riding with ten to twelve hours in the saddle each day. Alone, or with one American companion, there would be two mozos and two or more pack animals.

Among pleasant memories are nights spent by the trailside, the sound of music from nearby fellow travelers, arrieros who are also camping for the night beneath the big trees and bright stars. With one guitar or more, items which almost every pack train carried, they sat and lounged round the campfire as the rhythmic melody of music and song blended in harmony with the environment. Playful, with an occasional sharp quip and laugh or curdling Indian yell, they represented more than anything else I know of, the freedom-loving, independent spirit of their race. Also, they offered a soothing prelude to a full night of sound sleep!

Good arrieros seldom object to walking. A 15-mile hike on the trail to them was comparatively "easy work." Yet, let not the unassuming, carefree disposition of these simple lads lead you to conclude they are lacking in merriment and skillful humor. The

*Parker, left, wrote that among his
more pleasant memories were nights spent on the trail.*

schedule of the trail must be maintained, or so you think. Woe betide the late sleeper, that tenderfoot who allows his barefoot mozos to break camp, load up, and take the lead on the trail ahead. Once there, they will stay unless immediately checked and told to get behind and follow. Never was admonition more justifiable: "Get thee behind me, Satan." Once ahead and allowed to go, away vanish the bedding, grub, mozos and mules, except possibly for a fleeting glimpse on some far distant ridge. There is no use trying to catch up for they can travel faster than you can, and they know it. For a snack to eat, a place to rest, the daylight chances are ninety-nine percent against you. Finally, perhaps an hour or so after dark, weary, sore and *mad*, arrival is made at the place selected by them as night-camp. With a fire blazing, the mozos are indifferent or else they pretend concern with a bland statement that they themselves have been there since two hours before sundown. However, there is a big pot of hot coffee and supper is prepared, so there is nothing to do but to eat. The jokee may not readily see the joke, though memory of that day's journey provides a lesson not soon forgotten.

The muleteer is rated by his ability to deliver by the means at his disposal, despite impending obstacles. Slowly and patiently they plod day after day uphill and down, packing, driving, unpacking ornery Mexican mules. They have only one object in mind, and that is the successful delivery of cargo. Hard-working, persevering, determined, quick on the trigger no matter what the occasion, such are the qualities that make the life of a muleteer a strenuous one. They are fearless, reckless at times, but once started, they are hell-bent to go and to deliver.

Headquarters, and home for all three of our boss mule packers, Juan Chávez, Pascual Orozco, and Pancho Villa, was Guerrero, a small village north of Miñaca. As contract packers they controlled all transportation throughout the Ocampo, Rayón, and other districts of the Sierra Madre. Every trail and settlement, nook or hideout was to them about as familiar as their own backyard. Hard-working, dependable, with hundreds of men in their employ and thousands of mules and aparejos, they handled a job that required a tough personality, a rugged physique, and courage and brains. Hence, because they were organizers of men and transportation, and dauntless, hard fighters, they possessed the qualities of a generalísimo.

The number of men and mules engaged does not mean that they were men of wealth. Many of the arrieros were sub-contractors from small ranches in the neighborhood, while most of the mules and aparejos were rented from the larger haciendas. The contractor's job was to streamline and make delivery: Chávez with bullion, Orozco mainly with arrangements and packing the cargoes at Miñaca, Villa back and forth on the trail to keep the pack trains moving. Well known, friendly with all the officials, unafraid of anything or anybody, fair in their dealings, they were a trio whose influence with the mountain people of western Chihuahua was second to none.

The revolution headed by Francisco Madero was launched November 1910 in the state of Coahuila, east of Chihuahua and not far from the city of Monterrey. Jumping the gun somewhat earlier than the date set for it to start, the first real fighting occurred near Guerrero and Miñaca. It was led by La República's three boss mule packers, Orozco, Villa, and Chávez, as head of the insurgent forces. Madero, thus forced to show his hand, with an escort slipped across Chihuahua on horseback and joined this uncouth, ill-equipped group. Since success crowned their first foray, they soon took over the Rural garrison at El Valle, defeated a company of Federal troops from Chihuahua City, captured Casas Grandes, then continued north and assaulted and took the city of Juárez, opposite El Paso, on May 8–10, 1911.[1]

Advance and retreat was the game, with the latter being mostly for food and rest. Madero, who with Orozco and Villa was hiding out in the hills across from the El Paso smelter, entered Juárez and took possession. Madero reaffirmed the appointment of Abraham González[2] as governor of the State of Chihuahua. That same day, with a pass from the new governor, one of the first issued,

Mrs. Parker and I crossed the line, to view the wreckage. We saw plenty of evidence of the fierceness of attack and resistance. Deserted houses, broken windows, crumbled walls, gaping holes between rooms of adobe houses, indicated that advances were made "under cover" instead of along the streets. Splashes of blood were still on the sidewalks, and bodies were being carried to the cemetery for burial. The streets were fairly deserted except for small detachments of rebel troops led by escorting officers. Each soldier carried a rifle and four belts of cartridges, two around the waist and one diagonally suspended from each shoulder. Uniforms were noticeably lacking as the common soldado was dressed in overalls, a shirt, sombrero, and sandals.

On our visit we met and talked briefly with both "President" Madero and "Governor" González. The latter, standing in the entrance doorway of the Federal Building, spoke in a crisp, forcefully suppressed voice, yet with energy, confidence, and understanding of his position. He was giving directions and orders to civilian officials of the various departments of his newly acquired office.

The only souvenir we acquired was a small crucifix, which came from a soldier lad whose age could not have been more than fifteen years. Like all the others he was proudly bedecked with four belts of cartridges and a rifle, with the crucifix pinned to his dirty shirt. Obviously, it did not match the balance of his costume. Noting our attention focused on the ornament, true to national and native instinct, he handed it to us as he insisted, *"de Uds., vosotros! Su seguro servidor"* (For you! I am your servant). Despite our protest and refusal, he insisted, though he would neither tell where it came from nor how he got it. We still have the crucifix. For him, was it an heirloom or a token of war?

Gen. Juan J. Navarro,[3] the federal commander, was taken into custody when the town surrendered, but he was later released by order of Madero and escorted to a point below town where he crossed the river to the United States. His second in command,

Col. Manuel Tamborrel,[4] did not fare so well; he was killed during the last moments of action.

Among the Maderistas attacking Juárez, some four hundred all told, were about sixty foreigners, mostly Americans. Included on the list were at least four men whose faces were familiar in El Paso. One of these, Giuseppe Garibaldi,[5] was the grandson of the famous Italian patriot. A few years later, during World War I, he became a general in the Italian Army. Another prominent Maderista was a rancher at La Mesa, near Las Cruces, New Mexico. This was Benjamin Viljoen,[6] who had served as a general in the Boer War and as Chief of Staff under President Paul Kruger. He left the Transvaal when the British took control. Capt. Oscar Creighton,[7] an American, was perhaps the most typical of them all. He was a trusted friend of Madero who specialized in blowing up bridges and destroying railroads. His devilry made headline news until shortly after the fall of Juárez when he was killed in action, perhaps mistakenly by one of his own men.

The fourth fighter, Col. Emilio Kosterlitzky,[8] was a Russian, the son of a Cossack officer. He had served in the United States army, and had been appointed by Díaz as colonel of the Rurales in Sonora, with headquarters at Cananea. Kosterlitzky was a colorful figure in Mexican politics and the dreaded scourge of all who possessed even a suspicion of outlawry. The story circulated freely that the colonel was a wild, arrogant, and fearsome character. Wherever he went the people doffed their hats and disappeared, fearing what he might do next. When the Madero revolution started, he was at the head of his company of Rurales when he sallied out to annihilate the Maderistas. Leading the charge, the mule he was riding became frightened, bolted, and ran directly into a band of insurgent Maderistas. With escape impossible, he changed his allegiance pronto, and, without dismounting, he led the rebels back against his own Rurales, who, seeing their commander on the go, joined in the race joyfully shouting "Viva Madero." I understood he was coldly received by Madero and other officers when he arrived at Juárez, a day or two late, after the surrender of that city several months later. Nevertheless, around Cananea he was considered *Bravo del Macho*, "brave on a mule."

To get back to our muleteers and generalísimos. Juan Chávez, a bullion contractor, Pascual Orozco, a cargo contractor, and Pancho Villa, a trail boss, were among the first generalísimos appointed by Madero in the revolt against President Díaz. At the outbreak of hostilities we had reason to believe all three issued orders that La República mine not be molested. Later, when cargo on the trail became the coveted prey of irresponsible and irregular bands of guerrillas, the influence of their protection was practically nil.

Juan Chávez was fairly well educated and the chief of them all. Blind in one eye, with the eyelid closed, his most noticeable feature was the other eye. It was unusually large, round, and sharp, and he could see quicker, better, and farther than most men could with two. He was tall, stout, and had a heavy frame filled with energy. A bull's eye shot with either rifle or revolver, he was a near-perfect type of buccaneer, big, alert, and fearless. He possessed such a strong character and loud voice that he was much more of a leader and fighter than either Orozco or Villa. Had he lived, he undoubtedly would have been the *jefe*, chief military leader of the rabble-revolutionary forces. He was killed during one of the early skirmishes with federal troops near El Valle in 1911.

Pascual Orozco had only a slight education but was medium tall, well built, and aggressive. Early in 1911, when Madero left Juárez for Mexico City to assume the presidency vacated by Díaz, he left Orozco in command of all the military forces of northern Mexico. Failure for several months on the part of Madero to provide the necessary funds to pay his soldiers resulted in a visit by Orozco to the capital, where, at the point of a gun, he not only received the money asked for but a definite promise of no delay in future monthly requirements. The news spread so rapidly that Orozco was for a time considered to be the strongest, most powerful political figure in Mexico. The bubble burst in December 1912 when, fed up with broken promises, Orozco revolted. Little did he realize the gravity of his defection, that he was definitely playing into the hands of the enemies of Madero.

In the meantime, in southern Mexico Félix Díaz,[9] nephew of ex-President Díaz, encouraged by his uncle's friends and politicians, was vigorously staging another insurrection, one financed by the Church and other big landowners of that region. Madero, ever a weak man, a dreamer, inexperienced in politics, finance, or administration, had been since his arrival at the capital a tool of false adulation. In desperation he turned for assistance to Gen. Victoriano Huerta, former Minister of War and close friend of ex-President Díaz, who, offhand, was appointed by Madero as war minister and commander of the entire Mexican army. The logical and nationwide anticipated result followed. Huerta lost no time in playing the high cards thus dealt to him, in trust, by Madero. Within a couple of months, Madero was deposed and assassinated. Huerta assumed the presidency. In the meantime the revolt of Orozco was crushed. Crossing the line into Texas several months later as a cattle rustler, he was shot and killed by Texas Rangers.

Pancho Villa, uneducated, taught to read and write in later life by his wife, was an outlaw since early manhood. His real name was Doroteo Arango, and his parents were small farmers near El Valle. Villa, himself, was a vaquero on a hacienda in the neighborhood. The story as told to us at La República was that on learning that his sister had been ravished by the local capitán of Rurales, he rode into the barracks, shot and killed the capitán, then escaped into the mountains west of Guerrero. Protected by friends, and no doubt because of the popular decree of justification for his act, the matter was dropped.

He was known henceforth as Pancho Villa. As I knew him, he was a good worker, a go-getter, trustworthy, and dependable. During and after the revolution he was known as "a friend of the common people" and the "Scourge of Mexico." When Orozco revolted against Madero, Villa remained loyal. Driven by Orozco from his temporary headquarters at Juárez, Villa crossed the line to El Paso where for several months he lived in exile in a two-story brick house diagonally across the street from our home. Well dressed and respectable, he frequently walked downtown with me.

On returning to Mexico he joined forces with generals Alvaro Obregón and Venustiano Carranza and led most of the fighting near Mexico City that drove Victoriano Huerta from the country. Carranza had experience as a former governor of Coahuila, so Villa conceded that Carranza was the logical man to succeed to the presidency. Carranza was affirmed, and there the trouble started. The new president appointed Obregón secretary of war, with Villa in a secondary position. To this Villa objected; he seceded and started a revolution of his own. In other words, he refused to be "pushed around."

Defeated in battle by Obregón (who lost his right arm in the fight) Villa retreated northward, looting and plundering wherever opposition was offered. The loot was distributed among the poor people of the towns and his own impoverished followers. For himself he kept little or none at all because money, to Villa personally, seemed to have no appeal.

Despite a violent temper, Villa was trusting and loyal, particularly among those whom he considered friends. A particularly close personal friendship was with Gen. Hugh Scott, commander of the United States forces along the border. After Villa's break from Carranza and Obregón, within a year's time he, with other rebel "chiefs," controlled more square miles of territory in Mexico than Carranza. Yet along the border where Plutarco Elias Calles led the only Federal force in northern Mexico, Villa, while hemmed in at Agua Prieta, acceded to and followed the suggestions (orders) of General Scott almost without question until the "recognition" by the United States of Carranza as the lawful President of Mexico. From that time on Villa had no use for Americans, and he was convinced that General Scott had double-crossed him. His answer was the unwarranted surprise attack on

Columbus, New Mexico,[10] of which he was in charge. The idea that General Scott was in any way concerned was merely another outbreak of his unpredictable mind. Adolfo de la Huerta (no relation to Victoriano Huerta) was named provisional president. During the few months of his administration he is credited with the pacification of Pancho Villa, who was still a thorn of discontent from his numerous hideouts in the mountains. The Sonora "triumverate," Obregón, Calles, and de la Huerta, came to have complete control.

Near the start of the Revolution one of Madero's first official acts was to appoint Abraham González as governor of the State of Chihuahua. At the time, González was a resident of El Paso, a customs broker for cattle and merchandise shipments in and out of Mexico. With offices adjoining Parker and Parker,[11] on the second floor of the old Masonic Temple building on San Antonio Street, we knew him well. A graduate of Notre Dame, Indiana, he was a cultured and highly respected man, speaking excellent English. His life and term of office lasted only about two years. Shortly following the assassination of Madero in Mexico City on February 21, 1913, González was deposed and placed in custody at Chihuahua City by the military, whose officers, newly appointed by Victoriano Huerta, were mostly pro-Díaz and anti-Madero.

A few weeks later, without trial and under pretense of protection, Mr. González was escorted to the end coach of the train going south to Mexico City. With no inkling of what was about to happen, a couple of hours out from Chihuahua City he was blindfolded and led through the aisle, ostensibly to be transferred to the coach ahead. In the meantime, the coach in which he was riding had been uncoupled from the one immediately in advance and was then running several feet behind, with an open space between. On reaching the platform, González stepped, or was pushed, into the intervening space and his body was run over and mangled by the wheels of the coach. Speed slackened, the car was recoupled, and the train stopped. Then the train backed up to where the body was lying. The rear car guard and officer in charge alighted and advanced to administer the *coup de grâce*, a pistol shot through the head of the already dead, or dying, man. The body was left unattended and alone alongside the track. At the next station word was sent back to the authorities at Chihuahua City to go out and get the body.[12] With the death of Abraham González, Mexico lost a valiant patriot, a true and loyal friend, and another dark stain was added to that era.

After President Madero was murdered on February 21, 1913, Victoriano Huerta became provisional president. William Howard Taft, president of the United States, as a matter of courtesy left the matter of recognition to his successor in office, Woodrow Wilson, newly elected and inaugurated on March 4. William Jennings Bryan was appointed secretary of state, and there followed a series of diplomatic bungling — "Good Neighbor Policy" and "Non-interference in Internal Affairs." One of the first directives issued by the new State Department was a short, concise letter of instructions to all United States consuls in Mexico to advise all Americans in Mexico to get out, and words to the effect that "the United States government has no intention of intervention, could not and would not protect their lives or property." One-page pamphlets were printed and freely distributed.

It so happened that I was in Chihuahua City at the time and, at the Foreign Club, saw and read one of those circulars. The following day Governor González and myself were on the same train en route north to El Paso. In the Pullman coach, sitting side by side, we conversed on various subjects and he drew from his pocket one of the printed pamphlets. Handing it to me, he asked, "Have you seen this?" I replied in the affirmative. He then asked, "What do you think of it?" With considerable shame and confusion I answered, "Not so good; I don't like it." Then I added: "Would you mind telling me your reaction?"

Turning in the seat, facing me directly, he replied with words that still burn in my memory, "Not a word as governor you understand, but, knowing you as I do, here it is: Mr. Parker, to my way of thinking that note is an insult to every American citizen." Gripping hard the end of the seat, with flushed face he continued:

"If, anywhere on earth, under any circumstances, your own government will not protect you, who in h--- will?"

Mr. González was not a profane man and this was strong talk for him. Continuing, he said: "Furthermore, this is the first mention in any official note I have seen wherein the word *intervention* has been used. Why bring that up?" They were sincere words by a friendly neighbor, expressions confirmed by me and perhaps all other thinking Americans in Mexico. It was just a couple of days after his return to Juárez from Chihuahua City, that Governor González was apprehended and deposed, supposedly by his own garrison. A short time thereafter he was assassinated. For several years, the Bryan letter and its effect and the uncertain attitude of the United States administration caused many chagrined and angered Americans to register at the British consulates. Before that time registration in Mexico was practically unheard of.

From 1914 to 1916, when Villa had almost complete control of northern Mexico, his headquarters were in Chihuahua City where he and his officers occupied the residence of Don Luis Terrazas. It was one of the finest homes in all Mexico. Don Luis, Sr., was a co-general with Porfirio Díaz during the presidency of Benito Juárez and, like Díaz, first distinguished himself in holding back the French invasion, and, later, in bringing about the expulsion and death of Emperor Maximilian. When Díaz assumed the presidency in 1876, Don Luis was appointed governor of the State of Chihuahua and, for services rendered, was given a large tract of land which by later expansion became one of the largest ranches on the continent. During the early 1890s, in line with the Díaz policy of checking and curbing authority and political strength, Don Luis was replaced as governor by Miguel Ahumada. Some ten years later Ahumada, in turn, was transferred to one of the southern states, and Enrique Creel,[13] son-in-law of General Terrazas, was made governor. Creel was governor at the time of the Madero revolt.

General Terrazas was a small man, little more than five feet in stature. His three sons, however, Juan, Luis, Jr., and Alberto, were of normal height and weight. Alberto, the largest, was near six feet and well proportioned. Naturally, since the family was pro-Díaz, they and their possessions were considered fair prey by the insurgent Villa and his followers.

The nation had been severely harassed by the changes in government for three years before word was received of the Villa revolt against Carranza. Then came the harsh atrocities and looting by the advancing Villa forces on their journey north from Mexico City. The Terrazas family, and others of prominence and influence who had not yet left, hastily crossed the line to the United States. Don Luis, Jr., manager of the Terrazas estate, decided to remain, hoping by so doing to soften the anticipated blow. It was a mistake for which he paid dearly as he was seized and held as a hostage in his own residence, one that was separated and more modern than that of his father. The first ransom demanded was, as I recall, $300,000 in United States currency. It was paid within the time specified. Instead of release and freedom as promised, however, he was merely liberated from custody and deprived of privacy with friends and servants. He was not allowed to leave the city. Within a few weeks demands for additional ransom were made.

Since the ransom was not paid on the date specified, Don Luis, Jr., was transferred to the military prison, where a noose was placed around his neck and his arms were tied behind him. Then, from a crossbeam, he was strangled until unconscious with the soles of his feet barely touching the floor. He was revived and a few days were allowed for payment, but it did not come so the torture was repeated. Because of the chaotic conditions, ready cash was hard to get on such short notice. His father and friends in the United States employed every means possible to get the money, but they were hampered by legalities and the transfer and other essentials of delivery. Meanwhile, the bodily torture of Luis, Jr., was the measure stick for delay in payment.

Several times during the nearly two years of captivity the above agonizing torture was repeated. Disillusioned, Luis, Jr., lived on, broken in mind and spirit, hoping that death might bring relief.

When it became evident to Villa that this source of revenue was exhausted, Luis, Jr., was allowed to "escape." Entering the United States across the Texas border, he lived but a short time thereafter.

I was well acquainted with Don Juan, oldest of the Terrazas sons, who was then living in El Paso, and we frequently ate lunch together. A short time before Don Luis, his brother, was liberated, he told me that to date their father had sent $850,000 United States currency to Villa as ransom money for Luis, Jr. Don Juan also told me that during the last round-up of cattle on the ranch in 1913, more than 85,000 calves were branded. Of horses, mules, hogs, and sheep, he did not know the exact number but reported it was "scores of thousands." These furnished revenue and supplies for the Villa cause and aided in prolonging the strife.

Because of the distance from Villa's headquarters at Chihuahua City, other ranches in northern Chihuahua fared somewhat better perhaps, but not much. What happened at the Corralitos, Beresford, Boyd, Hearst and other ranches was not known to me. All were severely stripped of both animals and produce, but had no recourse except for compensation that the invader might offer.

When in 1916, Gen. John J. Pershing invaded Chihuahua for the expressed purpose of pursuit and capture of Villa, he did so because of orders from Washington.[14] Personally, he was well versed in guerrilla and Indian warfare and knew the futility of using heavy American cavalry in an attempt to follow the small Mexican mule on the mountain trails west of Miñaca where the natives were unfriendly and where Villa had innumerable hideouts. Also, he knew that a reward of, say, $50,000 to any one of half a dozen local ranchers, or border Rangers, might have achieved results, but he had orders from Washington. The invasion and withdrawal of General Pershing from Chihuahua, and also that of Gen. Frederick Funston to and from Vera Cruz, apparently were political, not military moves. Except perhaps as field maneuvers for training troops, they were complete debacles. Whatever their intent and purpose so far as the United States was concerned, they afforded the Mexicans a triumphant laugh and big boost in their proud morale. They had licked the Gringos — twice — and could do it again, if necessary.

A comparison of Geronimo and Villa is of interest. With five thousand American troops across the line in 1885–86, nobody ever *captured* Geronimo, the Apache renegade. With nearly one half of the entire United States army in 1916, nobody ever *captured* Pancho Villa. Both, tired of fighting, voluntarily surrendered — *quit*.

During the revolutions, a sight that drew the most attention and comment along the border was the large number of new, modern rifles, belts, and cartridges with which the Mexicans were equipped. They had practically no artillery and only the officers carried revolvers, but, infantry and cavalry alike, no matter how worn and ragged the uniform if any, each had a modern rifle and three wide belts filled with cartridges.

In light of the strict United States embargo, where did they all come from, how did they get across the line? In conversation with a couple of Negro soldiers from the United States Tenth Cavalry who were patrolling the line near Douglas, in answer to my question, one of them said, "Nothin' strange about that. If you was workin' for $20.00 a month and somebody come along and offered you $25.00 to turn your head and look the other way for fifteen minutes, would you do it?" Asked how they would feel if they received orders to cross over and keep on going, the answer was a unanimous "Hey mister, we'd like nothing better — Mexico City, then on to Panama. Ten thousand men is all we need." "Yes, might be," I said, "then another half million to police the country."

Yaqui Indians
and My Escape From
Revolutionaries

SOME OF THE MOUNTAIN TRIBES never did submit to Spanish rule, nor, until quite recently, that of the Republic. Notable of this class were the Yaquis of Sonora, whose independence and inflexible opposition to both Spanish and Mexican rule dated back to Cortez and the first viceroy. For years they defied troops sent against them and were finally brought under control only by means of armored airplanes, a method of warfare beyond their ken. Even so, the terms of submission embodied a subsidy of thirty pesos monthly to each man capable of bearing arms. In my experience the Yaquis have long been considered the best Indian fighters of the country, rated superior to the well-known Apaches of New Mexico and Arizona. The Apache on the warpath inspired terror among his victims, while the Yaqui, always on the defensive until after the Madero revolution, apparently fought for the fun of it. The more fighting they had, the more fun, and it is said that they did not torture or scalp their prisoners.

About 1900 a New York concern[1] obtained a concession for construction of a dam on the Yaqui River in Sonora, by which thousands of acres in Yaqui territory might be brought under cultivation. In exchange for this the New York company was to receive a specified acreage of the land thus benefitted, plus an acreage fee for water supplied to future colonists. The Yaquis were not consulted before the contract, but the state authorities, by edict and public meetings, endeavored to explain what was being done. They issued instructions and peremptory orders that

Yaqui Indians who worked in the Sonoran mines.
Parker wrote below this picture in his photo album:
"Mountain Indians. Not to be pushed around."

all persons within the area affected claiming title to land covered by the proposed project should come into Hermosillo, the capital, to register their claims and thus protect their titles. Posted notices, which few of the Indians could read, were mostly ignored.

Delegations of Yaqui chiefs went to Hermosillo to explain the problem that the land was all communal, the property of the tribe, and was merely divided among the families of each settlement. Since this had been the custom for generations, individual titles were nonexistent, so the chiefs and leaders could not ask the people to give up their homes to any foreign interest. State troops sent against the Yaquis were routed in defeat. Federal troops followed and were annihilated, so the government finally planned a campaign of extermination. The prisoners captured were almost all elderly people who were too old to flee or fight, or women and small children. They were gathered in groups and deported to

Yucatán,[2] the southernmost state of the Republic, a coastal low-lying region representing the extreme opposite of the Yaquis' high altitude, mountainous country. It was a sentence that meant sure death to the Indians. Men of military age were given no alternative: they could die in battle at home or face a worse death by starvation, disease, and fever in a tropical land. It offered a powerful incentive to fight!

Strange and frightful tales were then in circulation of vessels at Guaymas and other western ports which were loaded with prisoners destined for Yucatán. They would leave, and after a few days at sea would return to port with none but the crew aboard. In 1907, on the trail from Miñaca to La República, I passed one of these deportations which consisted of about forty old men, old women, women carrying babies, and children ranging from mere toddlers to ten years of age. They were ragged, dirty, barefooted, emaciated, weary and tired and all were walking and herded along by an equal or larger number of mounted soldiers heavily armed and with belts filled with cartridges crisscrossing their shoulders and around their waists. Never to be forgotten is that picture, and the facial expressions of hopelessness, suffering, fear — the agony of despair. Progress was necessarily slow, but the group was constantly urged along, often prodded by the captor-escort. Outstanding was a single young "buck" in his early twenties. Around both ankles was a chain which allowed steps of about eighteen inches. The chain led up front and around his neck, while his arms and hands were tightly bound behind his back. A look of abject humiliation did not hide the fierce, burning hatred of his captivity and his captors. Reports were not uncommon that a number of Yaqui youths, after their arrival in Yucatán, escaped, and, like homing pigeons (except for weeks of barefoot travel), returned to their homeland and tribe in Sonora.

Later in 1914 I had an experience with the Yaquis that was none too pleasant. During that time Pancho Villa had the entire state of Sonora under his control with the exception of Agua Prieta, and the Yaquis were fighting alongside the Villistas. The plight of Federal troops was largely caused by the fighting technique and superior tactics of the Indians. I was then operating the Fortuna-North Tigre group of claims[3] adjoining the well-known El Tigre mine,[4] fifty-five miles southeast of Douglas and thirty miles east of Ysabel, the nearest railway station. Troops were moving in close and we were cautioned against traveling at night, particularly in the dangerous Yaqui territory. Trains between Nacozari and Agua Prieta were running only at non-scheduled irregular intervals. Word was received that a train would be going north to Douglas at nine o'clock next morning, which meant that if I wanted to be on it, I would have to leave the mine not later than midnight.

On a good horse, with rifle in scabbard, six-shooter and belt full of cartridges, I rode to the El Tigre where I was joined by a mail carrier, a Mexican who was a most welcome companion. On our way, about three in the morning, wearing heavy overcoats and gloves in the freezing cold, we were about an hour out as we approached the river, where we saw a campfire in or near the road ahead. The sight indicated either Yaquis or mine freighters who were up early to get warm. Riding at a slow gallop, we suddenly heard a sharp call, "*Alto*" (stop). Bringing the horses to a walk we advanced toward the fire, and as we did so, every big rock and stump along the way suddenly stood up and came to life! By the time we reached the fire we were entirely surrounded by twenty or more huge Yaqui Indians. A sentry, the one who had challenged us, took my horse by the bridle and, rather roughly I thought, commanded "*Bájate*" (get down). Despite our having shouted "*Amigos, Americanos*" several times, he continued to berate us soundly for not halting at once when ordered to stop, repeating that not coming to a dead stop might easily have cost us our lives, as he and his men had orders under such circumstances to shoot, then ask questions. By this time we were both afoot and separated, and only later did I learn that they let my companion go on.

First, taking my horse, saddle, and rifle, they unbuckled and took my six-shooter, spurs, watch, keys, pocketbook, knife, letters and papers, everything from all my pockets. Then, with an escort of a dozen or more men, they led me toward the river where there were several small adobe shacks. In one of these, with the door wide open and a charcoal fire burning in the middle of the room, were several Yaqui soldiers sitting or lying on the floor. I had hoped that they were leading me to an officer, but was soon disillusioned since there was no officer in the bunch. They were just a group of sandal-footed, blanket-covered, cold and dirty Yaquis, and because of what my presence did to them, they probably did not like me either!

As I stood outside, an order was issued for those inside to vacate. I was then told to *"Pase adentro"* (go inside). No one else entered and I was alone with the warm fire and a box to sit on. Aside from the "arrest," I got to worrying whether I would be able to make my train, since it would require several hours' hard riding to reach the station at Ysabel by nine o'clock. The night was dark, the floor of the room was dirt — dirty, dusty dirt — so offered no pleasant prospect for lying down or taking a nap. I sat awhile, noticed the fire die down to ashes, then walked, sat awhile, then walked some more. Suddenly, outside in the brush somewhere, a horn tooted the reveille. Morning light was starting to break. Involuntarily, I stepped outside to look and listen, and from each side of the open doorway a soldier with rifle, bayonet attached, swerved and blocked the way. *"Espérate adentro"* (stay inside) one of them said. I turned back and did just that! If the voice that cried *"Alto"* to me sounded like a fog horn, this one was more like that of a bulldog. Neither sounded friendly!

Half or three-quarters of an hour later, about sunrise, there appeared in the doorway one of the biggest men I ever saw. He was the "capitán," a big, well built specimen of manhood. In addition to size he had another noticeable feature — he was blind in one eye. That one eye, however, like that of Juan Chávez, our bullion conductor at La República, missed nothing. It was triple strong and penetrated far beyond ordinary vision. In his hand he held all the letters and papers belonging to me. After the morning salutation of *"Buenos días,"* he began asking questions and also scolded me for traveling at night. I told him who I was, where

I was going, and what for. Among my letters was one written by the chief of police at El Tigre to General Domínguez,[5] head of the Yaqui forces in Sonora, requesting for me a permanent passport through Villista lines. The capitán opened and read the letter. This evidently satisfied him for after a few more words he asked if I would join him at breakfast. I replied that I would be pleased to if the delay would not be so great that I should miss my train. He insisted, however, and we had a good meal, just the two of us. He then ordered my horse fed and saddled, and returned to me all the things the soldiers had taken earlier in the morning. Then he informed me that he would send an escort of half his troop of about one hundred men with me on the trail. This is one thing I did not want, and I explained it to him in my very best Spanish. Having received such gracious treatment from him and his men, I anticipated the same if I should run into a bunch of federal troops. The troops might not shoot at a lone traveler, whereas they would shoot at an escort. He smiled as he saw the point. In crossing the river, however, he had several of his men lead the way to see that I got across safely.

It was a crisp, sunshiny day by eight o'clock, and it was too late to catch my train, except (as usual) it might be late! The road west from the river for a mile or more was at the bottom of a big split in the overlying basalt formation which had 500-foot perpendicular walls on both sides. The width was so narrow in places that freight wagons could not pass. Galloping along this canyon, I ran right into a company of cavalry at a turn in the road. Happily, among the men near the lead was a young American Mormon with whom I was acquainted and who was acting as a scout and guide for the military horsemen. Hastily explaining where I had been the past few hours, I asked if General Domínguez was among the officers, explaining that I had a letter for him. To my surprise one of the party came forward saying he was that person. He read the letter, talked awhile, then, with a fountain pen from his pocket he wrote on the margin "Pass anywhere in Sonora" and signed his name. True to native etiquette, he, too, offered me an escort. Again straining my imperfect Spanish, which, however, with assistance from the Mormon guide merely caused a laugh among the officers within hearing distance, and with "good luck" as parting salutes, once more I was on my way, alone. Urging my horse on as fast as possible, I constantly scanned the distance for smoke from the northbound train, and, seeing none, surmised I was too late.

After my arrival at Esqueda I witnessed a demonstration of the speed of travel by Yaquis afoot. Within two hours the entire command of my Indian "captors" came marching in, having traveled 23 miles from the river. Evidently they had left their camp after the arrival of General Domínguez, at least an hour, possibly more, after I had left them. Traveling afoot, they arrived nearly as fast as I did with a good horse, but this to me was nothing new as I had observed the same thing on the trail in Chihuahua.

As I was eating lunch, the capitán came in with three of his officers. After shaking hands he introduced the others and we all sat at the same table. With a broad smile and extra twinkle in that one eye, he unmercifully referred to me as "his prisoner," the Americano who refused his proffered escort.

The object of my going to Douglas was to purchase and, if possible, arrange for the transportation of supplies which were then near the vanishing point and necessary if we were to continue operations. Already, for months past, the difficulty and danger of passing through the two opposing forces, federal and Villa, had been a complex problem.

All loose Federal troops were then hemmed in at Agua Prieta with Gen. P. Elias Calles, afterwards president of Mexico, in command. He was able to hold the town because of the "umbrella" protection afforded by Gen. Hugh Scott and the United States troops on the American side of the line who served rigid notice to the Villistas that in case of border fighting, bullets landing on American soil would be answered by American artillery. Henceforth, no more border fighting between Carranza and Villa troops occurred.[6]

Having met General Calles before, I had no hesitancy in going across the line for an interview. At the time of my visit, 1915, he was thirty-eight years old, medium tall, and rather heavyset, and he wore a short mustache. His bearing was not that of a trained soldier since he had been a schoolteacher in Sonora for some seventeen years before joining the revolution against Díaz in 1912. Once in, he could not get out, and he reached his present rank more by political prowess than military.

Headquarters were in a one-story adobe building near the center of town. I was led to his room where he was confined by a bad cold, and two officers of his staff were present. We talked for quite some time because the general apparently was very interested in the Tigre district where I was then operating. A passport such as I requested, covering all of Sonora and Chihuahua, was readily granted. Presently the conversation led to the Cinco de Mayo, a rich silver mine directly across the valley from the Fortuna-North Tigre. I knew it well.[7] Formerly owned by Col. Francisco García, officer and member of the Díaz party, this mine was listed among those confiscated by the new regime of Carranzistas. That Villistas now were in possession of it seemed of little moment. General Calles wanted me to take it over and work it, and he would make any arrangement to accomplish his goal. It was a temptation all right, but there were too many possible entanglements. My negative answer was based on a lack of money and the troubles I had in keeping my own property going.

Evidently the general considered the remark either as acquiescence or a counter offer with only the money condition unsettled. With a motion for me to follow, he got up, walked across the room and unlocked a door, and the four of us entered the adjoining room. There we saw seven or eight steel-copper bound trunks, one of which he unlocked and opened, and said "Help yourself to all the money you want. When do we start?" It was that simple! The trunk was filled with packets of paper Carranza money, most of which was newly printed and worth at that time $.12 to $.15 United States currency per peso. Other trunks were the same, he said. This was strong talk and I had to think fast. Finally I anchored on the argument that during twenty years' residence and operating in Chihuahua and Sonora I had made a strong point of avoiding politics and, as a foreigner and American friendly to Mexico and the Mexican people, preferred not to get mixed up now. I talked myself out of a tight spot and a fat job, one I did not want. There was, of course, a lot more to the conversation, in which the two officers joined, but luckily for me it broke up without ill feeling expressed on either side.

Equipped with passports from the ranking military-political officers of both sides, plus half a dozen from local officials, a somewhat prolonged and diligent search was necessary to find an arriero willing to take the supplies back to the mine. Finally, one was found who for *double pay* was willing to risk a burro train (not mules, for fear of confiscation en route) and "to make the attempt" to deliver. He received the regular price on leaving Douglas, the same amount if and when the cargo was delivered. He, the arriero, won, except for one burro load of flour and bacon which he said was taken by bandits. We strongly suspected the bandit was the arriero himself.

And that was the last for us at the Fortuna-North Tigre, because we shortly thereafter closed down the mines. Scouring bands of guerrillas were partly responsible, but not altogether. Food and dynamite were their coveted prizes, but they were not the only "chiselers." Customs, export charges on two carloads of ore and one of mill concentrates, paid on the trip to Douglas relieved us of 28 percent of the gross value of their metal contents. Carranza received 16 percent and Villa took 12 percent, an amount that represented four times the normal peacetime tax.

What looked like a suspicious follow-up of the recent pack train of supplies from Douglas was the entrance in camp a few days later of another band of roving guerrillas with, as per routine custom, a courteous request for food and dynamite. Vigorously, but not *too* vigorously, the letters of Domínguez and Calles were presented, but the capitán said they were "*No vale nada*," worthless. The raiders helped themselves, and on leaving, the capitán handed me his *vale*, IOU, also worthless. Enough was aplenty, so we decided to quit and get out if possible.

Our few American employees were sent ahead via El Tigre coach and train, leaving U. S. Wolfe, the mine foreman, and myself to close down, gather what personal and company belongings we most wished to salvage, and with a pack outfit head for the U.S.A. Under ordinary conditions it would have been simple, but by this time the region was already overrun, and fast getting worse, with troops and bands of guerrillas on the move. We were faced with strong probability of confiscation of animals and everything we had. The greatest danger was from small detachments posing as soldiers, but in reality independent bandits, to whom our outfit would be a big haul and easy picking. From them the best we could expect was a long barefoot walk because American shoes were first class loot. A capitalist gringo, barefoot in the brush, to them would be very comical, *muy cómico*.

Wolfe, a fine fellow, was one of the best to be found for a trip such as that ahead. The time was mid-winter and the weather was cold. With three pack mules to carry our beds, suitcases, and provisions and one mozo, we headed north and east through little traveled territory, away from the railroad, and therein made a mistake. Leaving camp early in the morning, we traveled all day over a rough, mountainous country. The trail was ill-defined and hard to follow and spotted with unmelted snow. Camp was made at a point overlooking the country ahead, but despite the cold, no fire was built for fear of attracting attention. It was a precaution for which we had a reason for congratulation. Across the valley on the opposite hillslopes, hundreds of fires were seen all along Pulpit Pass, our intended trail of the morrow. Far into the night, with my binoculars, we watched them moving about.

A week or two later we learned that what we saw and almost ran into was the main Villa army, 5000 or more strong, en route from Chihuahua to its invasion of Sonora. Pay of the Mexican soldier at that time was one peso per day ($.10 United States currency) and a twenty-five pound sack of flour a week, on which he was supposed to feed himself and family, if any, who usually trudged along behind the column. Fresh beef was supplied from cattle of the ranches which the army passed, so they usually had plenty of free fresh meat.

We concluded that this was not the right direction for our getaway travel, so we retraced the trail back to camp the next day. Then we decided to go west of Agua Prieta. However, there in camp, we were detained a solid week by an unusually heavy fall of snow four to five feet at our camp in the mountains, and rain in the valleys, all of which made for a most disagreeable seven days. Having previously disposed of all the food stuff in the company store except what little we had saved for the trail, we ate with our Mexican caretaker, whose house was a dirty, filthy hovel. The last few days we ate canned goods from our pack and dirty tortillas furnished by the Mexican housewife. For our intended trip we boiled a lot of potatoes, had the Mexican woman make a big stack of tortillas, and made preparations with realization that a fire built anywhere along the trail might draw unwelcome attention.

Wearing our six-shooters only, we decided to conceal our rifles in the bed rolls on the pack animals. We thought that if we should run into soldiers and they saw no rifles, we stood a better chance not to be shot at, and, in a verbal argument could better show we were not mixed up in any of their military affairs. Also, each of us carried a pair of wire cutters, anticipating a barbed wire fence en route that might be an obstruction for a shortcut somewhere on the trail.

With the same outfit as that of the previous attempt we left camp and arrived at the river about two in the afternoon, where we found that the high waters from the storm had carried away the cable supports for the small boat ferry. This meant swimming our animals and making two trips with the baggage. On the west shore we were met by an American, Walter Hewitt, who was in charge of some thirty horses belonging to a friend of ours, Frank Whalen. Hewitt was endeavoring to get the horses across the United States line to prevent their falling into the hands of roving bandits or soldiers. With a Mexican helper he had driven them north and almost into the same big force of Villistas we had met.

Some of the horses were bred stock, so their loss would mean a lot to Whalen. Hewitt, in a bad spot, was fearful of losing the entire bunch. Since we decided our chances might be better than his, we exchanged our three pack mules and the horse our mozo was riding for four of his picked animals. The hunch proved right. A couple of days later Hewitt was forced to give up all of his herd in exchange for Villa money on a basis of about $3.00 United States currency per head.

With us, the next four days was a case of seek-and-hide as we zigzagged across country and followed no roads or trails except for short distances. The terrain over which we traveled was favorable for our purpose since it was made up of rolling hills and had no wide valleys nor wide open spaces. It had many small trees and a fair amount of mesquite and sagebrush. I would go ahead for a half mile or so, ride part way up some prominent hill, get off my horse and walk to the top where, with binoculars, I could scour the neighborhood for sight or evidence of "soldiers." With the way clear ahead, progress would be made in that direction. It was an exasperating and tiresome position.

One night we had a close call. Going up one of the wider valleys we turned into a side gulch, up which we traveled about half a mile. Then we went into a secondary gulch where camp was made for the night; our animals tethered in a parallel gulch over the ridge. We had eaten supper and were lying down, when, shortly after dark several shots were heard. We concluded that we, or our horses, had been sighted and followed. Wolfe and the mozo, with their rifles and plenty of ammunition, went over the ridge where the horses were, came back and reported the horses all right except for a slight restlessness caused by the shots we had heard. As a precaution, however, the two took a blanket and remained near the horses all night, while I stayed with the camp and other belongings. Early the next morning, the binoculars plainly showed smoke of two or more fires at the junction of the two valleys below where we were camped, about .5 mile distant. A ground view was impossible on account of an intervening ridge,

beyond which the smoke was visible. We camouflaged our equipment, saddles, and baggage by means of dead branches and brush,
led the horses farther back in the hills, and waited. About ten
o'clock they were brought back, saddled, and packed. Retracing
our trail of the previous evening, we cautiously approached the
junction of the gulches below, carefully watching a number of
buzzards flying overhead, and noting that they lit at the point of
observation, thus providing evidence that whoever had been there
was gone. Riding past the suspected point we saw the carcasses
of two steers and the general litter of a good-sized camp. The shots
we had heard the previous night were thus accounted for. We
estimated there must have been forty to fifty men camped there
during the night.

It was Sunday morning, and the sun was bright and clear. We
did not know just where we were, but thought the United States
border could not be far distant. Riding well ahead, I dismounted
near the top of a hill, got the binoculars into play, and soon was
overjoyed by seeing a long line of posts and fence wire running
across the flat at a right angle to the direction in which we were
going. Upon scanning the line, I saw two horsemen riding westward on the Mexican side of the fence. Evidently they were line
riders patrolling to prevent smugglers, deserters, and others from
crossing the line. I figured, at the rate they were traveling, they
would reach the nearest point of the fence from us at about the
same time we would, so I suggested we wait half an hour. Not so,
Wolfe. After all this he was not going to be stopped by a couple
of Mexican line riders.

Although it was a foolhardy thing to do — and in case of any
shooting it would have been an international question — we determined to move across that line, Mexican revolution or world war
to the contrary notwithstanding! The bed rolls were untied and
our rifles were taken out. After inspecting both rifles and six-
shooters, the scabbards were strapped to the saddles, rifles were
inserted, and belts and pockets were filled with ammunition. The
packs were replaced and we were ready to go. Figuring the line

riders would have passed the point of our objective, I took the lead, riding slowly as we emerged from the valley onto the open, gently sloping plain. We went not too fast because we could still see the two line riders slowly going west, though they had already passed the point for which we were headed. When we were about halfway to the fence, we saw them suddenly turn their horses and stop.

Drawing my 25/35 rifle from the scabbard and laying it across the saddle in front, I put spurs to my horse, at the same time waving to Wolfe to come on. The pack horses, urged by Wolfe and the mozo, took the case, and together we raised a lot of dust. With a sharp lookout on the two men on the hill, we loped toward the line as fast as we considered safe for not dislodging the pack from our horses. After a final spurt I reached the fence, dismounted, and cut the wires — and the next instant we were across the line.

What a grand and grateful feeling! The ozone of the air had a different smell. We were home safe and no longer on the dodge. We did not know it, but there was still more trouble ahead! The point where we crossed the line was about 15 miles west of Douglas, the legal port of entry, so we rode along the boundary fence on the U.S. side of the line toward Douglas, camping that night a few miles from town. There we had our first fire and hot food since leaving Fortuna camp. Next morning, on arrival at the customshouse, the journey and entry were explained, and we were told in no uncertain terms "Impossible."

Just two days before a rigid embargo had been clamped tight on all livestock entering the state from Sonora on account of the hoof and mouth disease. We would have to take the animals back across the line! This we wholeheartedly refused to do after five days of hardship travel, plus seven days since the actual start. We had taken twelve days to cover only 55 miles, direct distance, and that was enough! Tempers flared on our part, but the officers remained adamant. American citizens, constitutional rights! If they wanted to drive our horses back across the line they could do it themselves; we absolutely would not. What a mess!

Dust-covered, dirty, unshaven, tired and hungry, we were in no frame to compromise, and neither were they. Finally, on my insistence, telegrams were sent to both Gov. George W. P. Hunt[8] of Arizona and Gov. William C. McDonald[9] of New Mexico, both personal friends of mine. The customs official doubted the truth of this statement, but by noon replies were received and the controversy was cleared. The animals were placed in the United States quarantine corral in Douglas for ten days' observation.

Then followed a hot bath, shave, change of clothing, and the best meal that the best hotel in Douglas, the Gadsden,[10] afforded. The episode of our escape still rankles owing to the fact that we were delayed in entry to our own United States homeland; it remains a thing to remember — a thorn in the flesh!

Mexico is a land of charms, offering many contrasting thrills. The trails, however, are sometimes rough, and although the writer has a kindly feeling for the people in general, when they are in revolt he has a strong preference not to be in the midst of the mix-up.

After the Revolution:
Los Tejones, Nayarit, and
Cananea, Sonora

SEVERAL YEARS AFTER THE MEXICAN REVOLUTION and World War I, mining interests again attracted me to Mexico, this time to Los Tejones, a property about 150 miles south of Mazatlán and 7 miles east of Yago, a Southern Pacific railway station on the north bank of the Santiago River. It was one of several mine projects on the West Coast financed by a group of wealthy Japanese, among whom the name Yamamoto[1] (the future admiral of the fleet) was frequently mentioned. Through a representative of their Los Angeles office I was engaged to make an examination and report. Leaving Los Angeles on December 1, 1923, with M. K. Sasaka, resident agent who spoke good English, we, in due time, arrived at Mazatlán, where we were delayed several days because no trains were running south due to local revolution and prowling bandits in that district.

The mines were situated at the base of the mountain range in a region of dense jungle vegetation penetrable only by trails kept open by the daily passage of men with *machetes* cutting anew the fast-growing tentacles of brush and vines. The canopy of spreading branches and large leaves was so dense that sunshine seldom reached the ground; the air was stagnant, stifling hot, and enervating. Though the time of year was December, burdensome perspiration accompanied any sort of movement, day or night. If a breeze ever penetrated below that cover, I never saw, heard, or felt it. When it rained, no drops fell to the ground, only rivulets following channels in the dense canopy of leaves overhead. The mines consisted of a number of shallow workings, mostly old Spanish diggings. The Japanese had spent a lot of money, most of it on or near the surface, but obviously no experienced mine or mill operator had been connected with the enterprise.

There were two camps, Japanese and Mexican, about 200 yards apart, invisible one from the other on account of the jungle. In the Japanese camp, in addition to the mill, assay office, and warehouse, were two imposing pole-frame structures, each about 75 feet long by 30 feet wide. Each roof was closely thatched with palm fronds and ferns, and the slope of the roof extended beyond the sides of the building, thus affording high ceilings and side, cool porticos. They were the living quarters for the Japanese; inflammable, yes, but tight and comfortable. My room was in the assay office on the hillslope above the mill. The camp was well laid out, not crowded, and the varied green of the enclosing forest and jungle provided a picturesque background to the mixture of the native and modern architecture. The Mexican village was more typical of native structure, though it plainly showed the evidence of Japanese supervision. All the houses were built of round poles, and the walls and roofs were thatched. For daytime living quarters, with but a few exceptions, each house had its projecting portico, with built-up rock or adobe fireplace, hang-up forks or brush for utensils, saddles, and blankets.

My sleeping quarters were apparently one of the chief breeding and incubating places for fleas. The first few nights they simply came in droves. Luckily I found a remedy, a partial one anyway, that permitted me to sleep. Two quart bottles of Gordon's Gin, unopened, were on a shelf among the chemicals of the assay office. A good rub down at bed time, another one during the night, and another while dressing caused the itching and biting to diminish. I either became immune, or the fleas left for a less alcoholic feeding ground. Never have I known a better use for Gordon's Gin!

About twenty of the workmen in camp were Japanese, while about forty were Mexicans. Only one of the Japanese, the manager, K. Kimura, spoke fluent English, but the cook and one or two others spoke fair Spanish. All were notably superior to the Japanese labor formerly employed by me in Chihuahua and Sonora. At Tejones they did most of the surface and camp work, leaving the underground and mine work to the Mexicans. Wages were comparable to other camps of that region: one peso per day for common labor to four pesos per day for machine drill miners. Exchange was then about $.30 per peso.

A short distance from the cookhouse was a community bath out in the open with no house or cover. It consisted of a square wooden tank on a platform about a foot above the ground, and off to one side was an upright firebox boiler for supplying hot water. Having completed the day's work, all the Japanese took a daily bath, and they wanted it *hot*. No soap was permitted in the tank. If required for excess dirt or grease, to one side was a basin and shower for that purpose, to precede the bath. Bathing occurred in rotation without change of water except for replacing hot water with hotter water from the boiler. I was told to come first if I wanted to bathe, an intended compliment no doubt. Determined to prove I was not tender, I managed a little at a time to get in all over, to sit down covered to the neck, the same as the Japanese with only my head above the surface. But it was an ordeal. My mind reverted to cannibalism; a bit more heat and the sons-a-guns might eat man-meat for dinner! After a day or two I became more accustomed to the "torture" and returned regularly for more, but not hotter.

I had been at Tejones less than two weeks, and my initial work was not complete when anxiety and excitement came our way. The camp was raided by guerrilla mountain bandits, their first foray at Tejones. At nine in the evening, bedtime in camp, I was seated at the table in my room writing when I saw one of the Japanese come running up the hill shouting: "Out! Pronto out!" I only half understood and my uncertain movements were confusing as he ran off like a scared rabbit. Almost immediately the generator stopped and the lights went out; however, the moon was high and visibility outdoors such as only clear nights and tropical skies produce. With no time lost for tying it up, my bedding was carried to the edge of the jungle, twenty-five yards distant and thrown behind a fallen tree. Returning by aid of a carefully shaded flashlight, I packed my suitcase and took it with the bedding to another tree. In the dark shadows of the jungle, with Kodak, aneroid and binoculars over my shoulder, I sat down and waited.

From this position, there was a plain view of the road emerging from the jungle and leading to and between the mill and Japanese houses; a grandstand view of what, if anything, was to take place 75 to 100 yards from where I sat. Japs were seen running, disappearing into the forest jungle. Some carried suitcases and bundles, but others were just running. Suddenly, from a turn in the roadway, thirty or forty horsemen came racing in, yelling and firing. With the two Japanese houses surrounded, most of the men dismounted and entered, while two or three stayed with the horses and empty saddles. Others rode on to the Mexican village. The loud yelling stopped, and only an occasional shout, probably a command of some sort, was heard. Quick movements among the horsemen were apparent as articles were being moved from the houses for loading on pack animals evidently brought for that purpose.

Suddenly a single shot rang clear. Men came running and the excitement increased. Some mounted their horses to dash to and fro while others assisted the mule packers in loading cargo. Five men entered the mill while two horsemen encircled the building, passing close to the assay office to which they paid no particular attention.

Anticipating trouble and more shooting, I decided it was time to move. With my suitcase I went further back into the jungle. It was comparatively dark in there, but I kept on half-groping and stumbling for perhaps a hundred feet. I found a fallen dead tree trunk under which I shoved the suitcase. I crawled alongside and sat down and waited. Time dragged, a long time, probably half an hour, and no more shouting or shots were heard. And then, from the direction of the assay office a light was seen coming in my direction.

Alert, uncertain, behind the log with my baby five-shooter (a Smith and Wesson .32 caliber, the only firearm I had brought on this trip), I crouched. The light, a carbide lamp, came closer, zig-zagging, obviously searching, but the reflector kept me from learning an important item — the nationality of the bearer. When almost opposite me, the man stopped and I heard him call "pa-ca," "pa-ca" (Parker, Parker) at the same time that I caught a glimpse of his hat and features. His presence told me that it was all over the raiders gone. Apparently the shot heard just before I went back into the jungle was the bandits' signal for departure. Back in camp I met Kimura, who was apologetic that he could not have been with me. Sasaki, a few days before, had left for Mexico City

Hurriedly we went through the two Japanese houses. The bandits had done a thorough job of looting as the places were practically empty. The cookhouse fared but little better; cooking utensils, pans, pots, cutlery, dishes, all gone, as was the entire food supply from the storerooms. That they did not loot the main store and warehouse was a matter of uneasiness to the Japanese, who were fearful the bandits might return before daylight on a second sortie. My presence in the camp also was a disturbing problem because capture and ransom of American engineers was, at that time, a rather common and sometimes lucrative practice. Nobody remained in the camp. Kimura and I walked to a far side of the clearing where the trees had been cut for the sawmill and for fuel, to an elevated point above the mill. There we talked, dozed and finally slept. Breakfast next morning was in an adjacent hide-out with other Japanese, and it consisted of tortillas, eggs, and coffee brought from the Mexican village.

The vote being unanimous that I should leave camp, a horse was brought for me to ride and goodbyes were said. Then, with three Japanese to carry my luggage, I left. We did not go along the cleared trail or open road over which I had come into camp from the west, but we took another trail leading southeast, down the hill toward the Santiago River, two miles away. Kimura had sent a messenger ahead to arrange my transportation which consisted of a canoe, manned by a boatman and hidden by high grass and brush. No time was lost in loading, and with a few quick strokes of the paddle, we were off. The canoe was a common river craft of that region, a hollowed log pointed at the ends, about sixteen feet long with a three-foot beam and one center board seat. The boatman was an old-timer, an Indian, an impressive, silent figure who apparently knew all the tricks of the river.

Seated on my bedroll at the stern, speeded by the buoyancy of the canoe riding the current and the standing Indian expertly handling the paddle, alternately with and without my binoculars I noted our progress and watched the shore. It was a pleasant thrill as only a guiding dip of the paddle was used to keep the canoe straight on the rippling surface. For four or five miles the forest jungle continued close down to the highwater mark of the riverbank. Farther west the dense vegetation grew less, with occasional native dwellings, cultivated fields, a few scrub cattle, increasing in number as we drifted west. Until we passed the high, wide-spaced steel and concrete railroad bridge, one of the longest and highest in the republic, the Indian paddled with strong and steady strokes. Beyond the bridge the canoe was allowed to drift with only an occasional paddle-dip, a steering drag or push. His manner clearly showed relief of apprehensive tension after we passed the bridge.

The day was bright, the air clear and fresh, a welcome change after the jungle moisture and heat. Added to the changing landscape and varied vegetation, a fascinating part of the voyage to me were the dozens of alligators and iguanas (immense yellow-green lizards) along the shore. The former were like water-swept logs, often all concealed, and when aroused by our passing, they ran toward the river and disappeared in the water. For amusement, after passing the bridge, a shot from my five-shooter would cause one or more of the reptile varmints to exhibit their speed, which was amazingly fast for a belly-scraping, awkward animal.

The iguanas appeared well fed with their bright canary color blending with the vegetation and their tightly drawn skin reflecting the sunlight. Ranging five to six feet in length, they usually were seen on horizontal branches of trees close to the water, above reach of the alligators. As we passed, those nearest the canoe would raise up on their funny jointed legs, swell their bodies to the size of a barrel — very much like a desert horned toad — and spit with a whizzing, whistling sound in our direction. Some, after spitting, would crawl or jump to the ground and scamper off inland. Iguanas are practically harmless because they are not provided with armor or sharp death-dealing jaws and teeth like the alligator and they are vegetarians which feed on the luscious tender plant growing close to the water. No doubt they furnish many a balanced meal to the alligators.

Miles before we reached our refuge point the sound of church bells was heard, and it increased as we approached our destination. They served as a reminder that today was Christmas as they called the people for worship, reverence, and celebration. Some 20 miles from our starting point, four hours by boat, we arrived at Santiago-Ixtcuintla, a town of importance in that region. We landed about noon on a pebble-strewn beach at one end of a long line of women engaged in the family wash. They were a staring group, surprised by the canoe bearing an unexpected guest, an American. There was no welcome, no opposition, but obviously a lot of curiosity and ill-concealed excitement. Men and boys came running, our situation was explained, and two of them were designated to carry my luggage to the hotel. After a grateful exchange of adioses with the boatman, I followed the luggage.

On reaching the hotel, the *portero* (gateman) sent a mozo to advise the proprietress, who, after a friendly welcome, requested I sign the register. In the meantime the inquisitive crowd following from the river was told and retold the story of the bandits at Tejones. It caused no little excitement, and I was accepted as an escaped refugee. A mozo carried my luggage to the second (top) floor to my room, which was fully 16 by 20 feet with a 12-foot ceiling. The room faced the street and opened on the balcony overlooking the patio; it was big, clean, and comfortable. Warm water brought from the kitchen afforded a bath and shave. A clean shirt, "city" shoes, and clothes that needed pressing badly, greatly refreshed me. An appetizing lunch greeted my appearance downstairs in the patio even though the lunch hour was long past due. Such treatment tended to soften the extreme disappointment in the disruption of my personal timetable and affairs. I returned to California without incident, except for a memorable stop at San Blas,[2] the place where the Spaniards cast bells for distribution throughout the New World.

From 1925 to 1930 I lived in and near Cananea, Sonora,[3] a mining town of some 10,000 inhabitants, 35 miles below the border and 50 miles southwest of Bisbee, Arizona. In so doing I entered a hot spot of changed and changing conditions replete with evidence of their effect since the fall of Díaz. This was the period or rule and climax of the *Triumvirate* — Obregon, Calles, A. de la Huerta — during which the new constitution was rigorously put to work and the theme was "Mexico for the Mexicans."

To me the comparison of old and new was unfavorable, disappointing. Since management was no longer left to its own resources, industry was in the doldrums. A former school teacher, P. Elias Calles, was now the "Strong Man of Mexico" (President 1924–28), and his policies were largely fashioned by Vicente Lombardo Toledano,[4] the John L. Lewis of Mexico. Changing conditions all over Mexico were, no doubt, intensified at Cananea because of its proximity to the border, but the cringing attitude of the people toward government authority was no longer so plainly manifest. Neither was the former respect and welcome toward foreigners and foreign capital. Arrogance and demand were in the ascendancy.

The mines of Cananea were discovered and placed in operation by William C. (Bill) Greene, at a time closely coinciding with my occupation at Nacozari and Pilares, 75 miles to the southeast. These two were the largest copper production areas in Mexico,

with first-ranking Cananea still producing after 50 years of continuous operation. Pilares de Nacozari was second, but it was known during the 1920s as the highest dividend paying property of the entire Phelps-Dodge Corporation.

Despite long-lasting harassments of various kinds — labor, banditry, and changes in management — the mines at Cananea and Pilares continued to operate. During the middle 1920s several of Cananea's old abandoned drill holes were reopened and drilled deeper. The drillers found an immense new body of high-grade copper ore, one of the few large world deposits of almost pure chalcocite, copper sulphide, 80 percent pure copper.[5] Cananea stock jumped from $7.00 to nearly $200.00 per share before the depression came.

With the boom price of copper at $.28½ a pound after World War I, the depression of 1922 tumbled the price to nearly $.10 per pound. This was increased and stabilized by New York financiers at $.18 per pound and held there until the Big Bust of 1929. Then the price dropped to $.06 a pound, which, coupled with a $.04 import tax levied by the United States, caused the closing of the Pilares Mine at Nacozari in 1936. They simply could not operate on copper at $.02 per pound. Cananea, on the other hand,

Cananea, Sonora, 35 miles below the border and 50 miles southwest of Bisbee, Arizona. Stock jumped from $7 per share to nearly $200 before the depression.

because of the new ore body of 80 percent pure copper, continued to operate until the Anaconda Copper Company eventually secured control.

While at Cananea I made two trips in 1928 and 1929 to the well-known district of San Xavier,[6] some 250 miles south. The first was to check on a prospect, and the second was to examine and report on the advisability of continuing work on the principal mine there, Las Animas. From Torres, 30 miles south of Hermosillo, the area of San Xavier is about 90 miles to the east. A short distance from Torres were two of the best known old gold mines of Sonora, about one-half mile apart, with combined production said to have been at $80,000,000. The mines were situated in an isolated range of small peaks and rolling hills, and the most conspicuous features of the landscape were two enormous cone-shaped tailing dumps which covered several acres. At the time of my visit both properties were idle. The road east to San Xavier was across the desert, farming country and mountain slopes. It was a one-track road so infested with ruts, rocks, twists, and turns, that 15 miles per hour in the automobile was fast enough. Even so, travel per hour by auto was equivalent to that per day by saddle and muleback; seven hours by auto, seven days by mule pack train.

San Xavier on every side showed evidence of long time activity and prosperity.[7] Records of discovery and production went back some 200 years. About 1860 the principal mines were acquired and consolidated by a Chilean, Matias Alzua,[8] by whom high-grade ores from the Bronces,[9] Animas,[10] Santa Rosa,[11] and Nahuila mines were shipped by pack mules to Guaymas, the seaport on the west coast that was nearly 200 miles to the southwest. From there the ore went around the Horn to Belgium for smelting and refining. The second-class, lower-grade ore was treated on the ground by barrel amalgamation and the old time patio process.[12]

Following the death of Alzua, the mines were sold to an English company. About 1900, in separate groups, they were offered for sale; since that time they have been worked independently by different companies. In this vicinity, within a couple of days mule-back travel, were some other five or six mines in the million dollar class, but all of them except one, La Dura,[13] were closed down at the time of my visit. The Las Animas itself was in the final throes of suspension due to the new labor and mining laws, decreased revenue, and the inability to maintain development work ahead of extraction. A further source of harassment stemmed from frequent raids, particularly on the pack trains, made either by Yaquis or roving bands of free-lance guerrillas.

San Xavier, on the main trail, was the principal route between Hermosillo and the Yaqui headquarters farther east. The surrounding region was marked by the nationwide customary *mojoneras de muerte* (monuments of death), which were piles of loose rock two to six feet in height. The number of such mounds in this vicinity was plain enough evidence of factors which contributed to the difficulties of mine operations and the necessity of ingenuity, nerve, and ability to dodge corners as well as bullets in order to keep on producing bullion. The Yaqui revolt of 1905 and other outbreaks since that time no doubt accounted for many of the mounds.

A case in point was the manner by which one irate gringo out witted the treasure-snatching hijackers. Prior to the Madero revolution in 1910, and for a few years thereafter, the wagon road from Torres ended at the base of the mountain 8 or 10 miles before reaching San Xavier. From that point all cargo was carried to San Xavier by pack mules, and it was a section of road most frequently utilized by highwaymen intent on loot and a quick getaway and hideout. During certain outbreak periods it is said that the producing mines lost in supplies and bullion at least fifty percent of their production.

In 1911 the Schroeter-Laughlin[14] lease went into production, and after a couple of their pack trains loaded with silver bullion had been added to the 150 years' record of similar bandit expropriation, friend Schroeter worked out a simple and effective change of tactics. Heretofore the bullion had always been shipped as 100-pound "bricks," or bars, because they formed a convenient cargo for muleback transportation. Instead of casting the bars in molds of 100 pounds, a shallow hole was dug in the ground alongside the furnace (smelter), into which the bullion was poured in rough chunks or slabs of one ton each. By means of a sled or low two-wheel carts, these were dragged over the mountain trail, loaded on a wagon, and hauled to the railroad. The ingots were too heavy for man or muleback or a quick getaway, and only once was the cart held up. It was sidetracked down the hillside, demolished, and abandoned, but the bullion was left because it was too heavy to carry away.

The problems connected with the mines were insurmountable for me as it became more and more apparent that foreign capital and free enterprise were doomed in Mexico. I tried again in 1932, driving down the west coast to the ancient mountain town of Sinaloa, but it was no use. The mules and mines could not be worked, so Mexico was no longer for me.

Notes

EDITOR'S INTRODUCTION

Notes to Pages xiii–xx

1. Sonnichsen, 1971, pp. 2–3.

2. *Old Abe Eagle*, June 8, 1893; *New Mexico Interpreter*, October 11, 1889; *White Oaks Eagle*, March 26, 1896.

3. Sonnichsen, 1971, pp. 57–58, 77–78.

4. *Old Abe Eagle*, January 26, 1893, and November 22, 1894.

5. *White Oaks Eagle*, December 19, 1895.

6. J. B. Slack, Record of Deaths at White Oaks and Vicinity from 5–15–80 to 7–3–1905 (Ms.).

7. Leonard, 1925, p. 1596.

8. McNeely, 1964, 1ff.; Pletcher, 1958, pp. 22–27.

9. Bernstein, 1965, pp. 32–33, 36–41.

10. Griggs, 1907, and 1911; Bernstein, 1965, pp. 72–77.

11. Leonard, 1925, p. 1596; Sonnichsen, 1971, p. xx.

GUANACEVI, DURANGO,
AND THE BARRANCAS OF CHIHUAHUA

1. Guanaceví, in the northwestern corner of the state of Durango, is situated on the eastern slope of the Sierra Madre at an elevation of 8,000 feet above sea level. It forms the center of a highly mineralized zone which includes the mines of Santa Barbara, Parral, Magistral, Santa María del Oro, Inde, Carmen, Topía, and Guadalupe y Calvo. As early as 1616 Spaniards were relieving the mountains of Guanaceví of their silver, but extensive exploitation did not come until near the middle of the nineteenth century. The earth on this section of the Sierra Madre is a light grey, tufaceous capping that varies in thickness from one to five hundred feet. The capping is not mineral bearing, but where it has eroded sufficiently the minerals can be found. At Guanaceví this erosion had exposed three large parallel veins of silver each about two miles long. Upon these were two hundred separate mining locations by 1883.

   Guanaceví's big boom came in the mid-1890s as American capital pushed into Mexico. This was the exploitation that led Parker there, and it continued incessantly until retarded by the revolution in 1914. The area had plenty of ore, water, and wood, and its climate was nearly ideal; the problem was accessibility. Roads were so poor that the ore had to be transported out on muleback to either Mesa Zandia on the Parral and Durango Railroad or to Rosario on the Mexican Central Railroad. As late as 1911, just before the shutdown, reporter R. G. Kline explained the problem: "At present ore or concentrates must be hauled 75 miles to the railroads, but there is a good wagon road and the trip is made in 1½ days." That good "wagon road" was not built in 1895 when Parker was there, so there should not be wonder that he felt the sting of primitive living conditions.

Source: Nelson, 1903, pp. 697–98; Kline, 1911, pp. 402–5; Graham, 1911, pp. 33–34; Dahlgren, 1883, p. 152; Rouaix, 1946, pp. 183–84.

2. In 1895 the state of Durango was comprised of 38,020 square miles and had a population of 294,366 persons, or 7.7 persons per square mile. It is bounded on the east by Coahuila, west by Sinaloa, north by Chihuahua, and on the southeast, south, and southwest by Zacatecas, Jalisco, and Nayarit. The western part of the state contains a portion of the Sierra Madre range which has peaks rising to 10,000 feet above sea level, while the elevation gradually slopes to the east until the terrain becomes plains dotted with treeless mountains. The only river worthy of the name in the entire state is the Nazas, which flows eastward from the Sierra Madre. The state's isolation made transportation facilities slow in coming and caused the difficulties Parker experienced.

Source: Romero, 1898, p. 91; Terry, 1947, pp. 401–3.

3. The Concord was a generic name for a stagecoach, so named for the town in New Hampshire where many of the coaches were made. Abbott, Downing and Company made the deluxe vehicles, which had the body suspended on leather thoroughbraces. Woodwork was hickory, metalwork steel and brass. Inside were three lines of three seats each, two facing forward and one back. Three additional passengers could ride on the roof. A small storage compartment was located under the driver's seat and a larger, canvas covered one was at the rear. The driver sat on the off (right hand) side next to the brake handle and the guard or swamper sat on the left. When protection covered the windows, it was of canvas.

Source: Rowse, 1976, pp. 1–9; Watts, 1977, pp. 95–96.

4. This branch of the Atchison, Topeka and Santa Fe Railroad was completed to El Paso on June 11, 1881. San Antonio, in

Socorro County, on the banks of the Rio Grande, has always been a good place for irrigation, thus fruits and vegetables are raised there in addition to cattle. Its spot on the river saved the town from being part of the famed Jornada del Muerto, a 90-mile waterless desert from Rincon to San Marcial, but the population has never been large. By 1910 only 434 persons lived there.

Source: Bradley, 1920, pp. 206–7; Twitchell, 1917, vol. 4, pp. 359–61.

5. Until July 1889, the town on the Rio Grande opposite present El Paso, Texas, was known as El Paso Del Norte. In the state of Chihuahua, its name was changed that year to Ciudad Juárez. The Mexican Central Railroad was started there in September 1882, when the population was estimated to be about six thousand persons. That same year saw the beginning of the El Paso-Juárez famed mule cars, like the one Parker rode. The original car is preserved and on display in El Paso. The bridge was built that year and service continued undisturbed until 1902 when electric cars were installed. By 1927 the population of Juárez was estimated at 19,457, so Parker must have seen a city of approximately 10,000 persons in 1895.

Source: Almada, 1927, p. 139; El Paso *Times*, September 28, 1921; El Paso Electric Company, 1921, pp. 2–3; Hamilton, 1882, pp. 148–49; Chávez, 1959, pp. 46–49.

6. In colonial days this town was Presidio de Guajuquilla, but after the revolution in 1811, it became Jiménez in 1832, in honor of Mariano Jiménez. The town is situated on a plain watered by the Río Florido. It is in the state of Chihuahua near the boundary with Durango. In 1883, twelve years before Parker was there, the villa became a station on the Mexican Central Railway, but it was not a large place, having a population of 11,246 in 1927.

Source: Almada, 1927, pp. 382–83; Lister, 1966, pp. 66, 88, 91, 195.

7. In September 1880, President Porfirio Díaz granted authority for the establishment of the Mexican Central Railway to a group of Massachusetts capitalists headed by Thomas Nickerson. The company was authorized to take any land necessary for the railroad's installation and was given an incentive of 9,500 pesos per kilometer of track laid. By April 1884, the company had completed its task, having built 1,224.2 miles of track. Mexico City served as the southernmost terminal and Paso Del Norte (Juárez) was the northernmost point. It became the greatest railroad in Mexico, one which eventually connected Mexico City with eight of the state capitals and extended its rails through sixteen states. In 1902, Henry Clay Pierce acquired control and held it until 1909 when the Mexican Central became a part of the National Railways of Mexico.
   Source: McNeely, 1965, pp. 14–15.

8. Walter D. Beverly, another mining engineer who visited Durango in 1892, described a similar experience. His trip was from Pedriceña to Durango in the same kind of coach. He wrote:

   Being awakened shortly after midnight, we entered the diligencia, which left at 1 a.m. to make a continuous run to the city of Durango. The stage was of the regulation Concord type, but the harnessing of the horses was novel to me. There were two wheelers, three "swings" and three leaders. Besides the driver there was a "whipper," who rode on the footboard, but jumped off and ran along with the team when whipping was required. Horses were changed every 15 miles and the stage made good time. There were nine persons inside, and every seat on top was occupied. I had a seat inside, which I chose as the more comfortable in the cool hour of the early morning when we departed from Pedriceña but as the day wore on I became very uncomfortable, and felt like a sardine in a tin box, so tightly were our arms and legs packed inside of the coach. We arrived at Durango at midnight, and I alighted from the stage with the feeling that 23 hours of continuous traveling in a diligencia with nine persons inside was an experience that I did not care to repeat.

   Source: Beverly, 1909, pp. 635–39.

9. Robert Stafford Towne opened the smelter at El Paso on August 29, 1887, and the following year, March 22, 1888, transferred ownership to the Kansas City Consolidated Smelting and Refining Company. There it remained until April 4, 1899, when possession changed to the American Smelting and Refining Company. When built, the plant had four lead blast furnaces and four hand roasters designed for processing lead and silver. Later, copper smelting works were added, but in 1895 the plant processed mainly lead and silver. It has been called the most important custom smelting works in the Southwest. For its history, see Vail, September 14, 1914, pp. 465–68, and September 19, 1914, pp. 515–18, and Lee, 1950.

10. The capital of the state of Aguascalientes, the town of Aguascalientes, is on the Mexican Central Railroad line from Juárez to Mexico City. Spaniards first visited there in 1522, but development was delayed until the seventeenth century when the hot springs and silver were discovered. The smelter was new in 1895 at the time Parker refers to it. Built by the Guggenheim family, the smelter was designed primarily to treat lead and copper, and had for that purpose four converters which would treat fifty tons of copper per day. Later the Guggenheims used this smelter as a lever to gain control of the American Smelting and Refining Company.

    Source: Bernstein, 1965, pp. 38–41.

11. Britton Davis, son of Texas governor Edmond J. Davis, entered the United States Military Academy on September 1, 1877. After graduating fourth in his class in June 1881, he served as a second lieutenant in the Fifth Cavalry for less than one month, until July 1, 1881, when he joined the Third Cavalry. Davis was involved in the Apache campaigns of 1884–85 and wrote a book, *The Truth About Geronimo* (New Haven: Yale

University Press, 1929), detailing his experiences. He was on leave of absence from the army after September 1885, and he resigned his commission on June 1, 1886.

By 1890 Davis was in El Paso interested in cattle and mines. In 1894 he went to Kansas City to promote the building of stock pens for El Paso, and the following year was involved in a large land purchase in Mexico between Juárez and the Samalayuca Hills, where coal was believed to be in large quantities. The plan was to build a railroad and develop the mines. He moved steadily to a position of prominence in El Paso, holding the titles of general manager for the Corralitos Cattle Company, the Candelaria Mining Company, and the Juárez Company. Until June 1901, the offices were in Juárez, Chihuahua, but in that month the companies moved to the third floor of the Coles Building in El Paso, where they occupied six rooms. Davis presented a paper to the 1902 International Miners' Association which he titled "Investments in Old Mexico" at about the same time that he added another title to his string, that of president of the Aventura Mining Company. In 1902 Davis served as chairman of the Mineral Collection Committee of the International Miner's Association, and he also worked for the founding of a first class social club for El Paso, one which stressed the need for good companionship and camaraderie to begin at four in the afternoon.

When the Juárez concentrator owned by the Corralitos Company was closed on January 20, 1904, Davis was asked how long it would remain idle. With typical brevity he answered: "It is closed down till they get ready to start it again." Perhaps there is no connection, but on March 5 of that year Davis became president of a new $1 million corporation organized under the laws of New Mexico. This was the Northern Mexico Development Company which claimed Alamagordo as its home office. The purpose of this organization was to operate mines in Mexico and the United States, but it specifically had two mines, the Aventura and the Santo Domingo, in the Sabinal mining district. Purchases of these mines were from the Candelaria Mining Company, a branch of the Corralitos Cattle Company, and Davis was general manager of both. He resigned from the Corralitos Company in 1906.

Perhaps this new company was what led Davis from El Paso. By 1929 he was living in San Diego, California, where he died on January 23, 1930.

Source: Heitman, 1903, vol. 1, p. 357; Porter, 1970, pp. 25–41; El Paso *Herald*, November 13, 1894, and August 20, 1895, and May 23, 1901, and January 18, February 3, 21, 1902, and January 20, March 5, 25, 1904; El Paso *Times*, April 15, 1935.

12. For additional information see Hodge, 1912, vol. 2, pp. 692–93, and Bennett and Zingg, 1935, and Cassell, 1969. Observations contemporary with Parker's are found in Lumholtz, 1903.

13. From 1631 to August 20, 1833, this town was known as San José del Parral, but on the latter date the name became Hidalgo del Parral in honor of the liberator of Mexico. Primarily it is known for its mining activities, for the cattle which graze on nearby hills, and for the murder of Pancho Villa on July 20, 1923. Its population in 1927 was 15,181, so it probably was smaller when Parker was there in 1895. Located just east of the Sierra Madre, Parral is approximately 150 miles south of Chihuahua City.

Source: Almada, 1927, p. 332, and 1968, pp. 252, 564–66.

14. George Eastman patented the name "Kodak" in 1888 and started issuing his famous camera. It was a small box $3\frac{1}{4}$ x $3\frac{3}{4}$ x $6\frac{1}{2}$ inches which was loaded at the factory with a capability of 100 shots. It cost $25.00, but had a disadvantage in that it had to be returned to the factory for reloading. In 1891 a new Kodak was sold which had removable film and was the

one that really brought on the camera revolution. Probably, this was the model used by Parker. Its cost new was $12.00, a figure so low that many were sold. By 1896 the Eastman company had created their one hundred thousandth Kodak.

Source: Hall, 1949, pp. 112–14; Ackerman, 1930, pp. 75–111.

15. This stream is a branch of the Conchos River. The Nonoava originates in a place named the Cerro Redondo, which is south of the pueblo of Humariza, and unites with the Conchos five kilometers north of the village of Nonoava. The principal villages along its banks were Humariza, El Ranchito, Huahuaral, San Cristo, Cienequita, and Nonoava.

Source: Almada, 1968, p. 363; Millares and Escribano, p. 18.

16. Probably this was the pueblo of Humariza which had at one time served as the site of the Jesuit mission, San Ignacio de Humariza, founded in 1667. Mines were found nearby in 1695 by an Indian named Lucas Ordóñez.

Source: Almada, 1968, p. 258.

17. This is San Francisco de Borja, located at the confluence of the Hacienda and Saquarichi rivers. It was founded by Jesuit missionaries in 1645 at a place the Tarahumara Indians called El Rancho Tehuácachi. It was destroyed in 1652 and rebuilt in 1676 by the Guadalajara y Tardá missionaries. Later the name was changed to San Francisco de Borja where 828 persons lived in 1927.

Source: Almada, 1927, p. 637, and 1968, p. 482.

18. This famous mining town was founded in 1687 by Antonio Rodríguez who established a mine he named San Bernabé. Later the town took the name Santa Rosa de Cosiquiriachi and still later it became Cusihuiriachi. Cattle are of some importance, but mining has always predominated. It had 3000 inhabitants in 1927, and 317 in 1959.

Source: Almada, 1927, p. 189, and 1968, pp. 129–30.

19. The city of Chihuahua, capital of the State of Chihuahua, is 225 miles south of El Paso. As the capital of Mexico's richest mining state, this city early became a center for mining interests and railroads. In addition, it also supports an extensive ranching industry. The American influence, primarily brought by men in search of mines, caused Chihuahua to be transformed into a modern city. Founded in 1709, the city had a population of 30,405 by 1900. Much of its history can be traced in the following: Logans, 1959; *Manual Informativo*, 1909; Lister, 1966; Almada, 1968, p. 139.

20. The Barranca del Cobre is a rift over 100 miles long, 5 miles wide, and from 4000 to 5000 feet deep. Since 1684 when the first white man, Father Salvatierra, descended into the famed Barranca del Cobre, it has been an awesome sight to the beholder. It is situated in the State of Chihuahua in the Sierra Madre country where the Tarahumara Indians live. Three of these barrancas — Del Cobre, Del Batopilas, and Del San Carlos — are on the western slope of the Sierra Madre and they cut a gap which runs generally in an east-west direction, thus impeding the progress of anyone crossing the mountains. Carl Lumholtz, who was there a few years before Parker, provided a picturesque description which equals Parker's.

    Source: Lumholtz, 1903, vol. 1, pp. 143–44; Lister, 1966, p. 47; Terry, 1947, p. 355.

21. Rising in the barranca country of southwestern Chihuahua, the Fuerte River falls rapidly to water the plains of Sinaloa before emptying into the Gulf of California. Its headwaters, the rios Batopilas and Urique, have a terrific battle with the mountains with the result that the gorges in the barrancas are spectacular sights. The Fuerte emerges from the mountains in the Barranca de San Carlos, a barranca that is between 4000 and 4500 feet deep and could be traveled in two days if it had a passable road along its bottom; however, the country is so rough that at least a week is required to pass through it.

    Source: Lister, 1966, pp. 3–4; Lumholtz, 1903, vol. 1, pp. 391–92.

22. Alexander R. Shepherd was born in Washington, D.C., on January 31, 1835. Between 1852 and 1870 he had established himself as "the leading contractor and real-estate promoter" in Washington and as such was in a position to participate actively in local governmental affairs. In 1871, when the territorial form of government was created for Washington, Shepherd became vice-chairman of Washington territory and *de facto* director of the board of public works. From that position he revolutionized the appearance of the nation's capitol, but in doing so he created numerous enemies. In 1874 a Congressional committee investigated his activities, remained silent about his honesty, and recommended a different form of government. When the new government was formed President Grant appointed Shepherd commissioner, but the Senate tabled the appointment. Shepherd went back into the construction business and remained in it until 1879, when he became interested in Batopilas. In 1879 he organized the Consolidated Mining Company with a capital of $3 million and his life was thereafter connected with the company. On May 1, 1880, Shepherd, his wife, and seven children, left for Mexico. The family rested for the summer at Chihuahua while Shepherd went on to Batopilas to begin work. He became a patriarch, but did not make the fortune he expected as most of the profits were invested in newer and larger machinery. Again his developmental instincts outdistanced his means, but where he found a primitive region populated by peons, "he left it well developed and with schools, hospitals, and all the other evidences of efficient leadership." Shepherd was still alive in 1898 when Parker was in the area, having had eighteen years to build his kingdom. He died in 1902.

    Source: Pletcher, 1958, pp. 182–218; Shepherd, 1938, pp. 1ff.

23. The line from Chihuahua to Cuauhtémoc was completed in 1900, but Cusihuiriachi was not connected to Cuauhtémoc until 1911. Construction on this line began in October 1910, and was completed by August 1911, when regular train service

began. It was intended to serve the mining interests at Cusi-huiriachi and in 1922 it became a part of the Mexico North-western Railway.

Source: Mexico Northwestern Railway Company (L. Roy Hoard Collection), p. 10.

24. Located 60 miles west of the city of Chihuahua, San Antonio de Arenales became Cuauhtémoc in 1900 with the arrival of the Mexico Northwestern Railway. It was named in honor of the last Aztec emperor. In 1922 and 1923 Cuauhtémoc became the center of a large migration of Mennonites, but at the time Parker was there the town was only a place for Indi-ans who operated a few *antigua* mines.

Source: *Estado de Chihuahua* (map); Almada, 1927, p. 183, and 1968, p. 126; Fretz, 1945, p. 13.

25. This town was for a time known as Muñaca, a corruption of the Tarahumara word "mayuyaca," meaning lion. Gradually the town name was changed to Miñaca and it became the record center (county seat) of the district of Guerrero. Prior to 1900 it was sparsely inhabited, but on May 20 of that year the Kansas City, Mexico and Orient Railroad reached it and a station was built on land James S. Clayton purchased from Simón Caraveo. It expanded until it had 500 inhabitants in 1927.

Source: Almada, 1927, p. 453, and 1968, p. 337.

26. Luis Terrazas' financial empire reached its height in 1910, just at the beginning of the Madero revolution. His estate was estimated at having from 5 to 7 million acres upon which grazed 200,000 head of cattle. Born on July 21, 1829, Terrazas carefully, very carefully, created his business holdings on hard work and good judgment. He married Carolina Cuilty on February 2, 1852, and the couple had twelve children. Between 1857 and 1866, Terrazas was often engaged in war, first as a constitutionalist, then as a Juárezista, and finally as an oppo-

nent of the French leader, Archduke Ferdinand Maximilian Joseph. Later he unhesitatingly fought a constant war with Comanches and Apaches. In 1862 he became governor of the State of Chihuahua, a position he held several times. Without doubt, he was the most influential man in Chihuahua during his lifetime, and in a land of big ranches, his was the biggest. The Madero revolution marked his downfall, so much so that he was forced to leave Mexico in 1913. Thereafter he lived at El Paso until 1919, when he moved to Los Angeles, California. He attempted to rebuild under the Obregón government, an endeavor which met with some success. When Luis Terrazas died on June 15, 1923, at Chihuahua, the place of his birth, he did not leave the survivors of his family as paupers.

Source: El Paso *Times*, June 16, 1923; El Paso *Herald*, March 28, 1903; Almada, 1968, pp. 523–26; Lister, 1966, pp. 140–56, 204–5, 229–32.

27. This phase of revolution began in November 1909, and continued intermittently until 1913 when Francisco Madero was killed. For details see Ross, 1955, and Cumberland, 1952.

28. Son of Luis Terrazas, Juan Terrazas was born in Chihuahua in 1852. He was a deputy in the Eleventh Federal Legislature, was a Senator in the state of Campeche from 1904 to 1908, and a deputy in the 24th and 25th Legislatures in the state of Chihuahua. Juan Terrazas was an industrialist, having a "tienda de raya" at the American Smelting and Refining Company plant near Chihuahua and a cement plant at Ciudad Juárez. The Madero revolution swept it all away, so Terrazas spent most of the revolutionary years in the United States. In 1916 he was reported to be supporting a revolutionary plot by Felix Díaz, but he published a denial. In 1920, Juan Terrazas returned to Chihuahua to assist his brother Alberto in rebuilding the Terrazas empire. They had some success before Juan Terrazas died in 1925.

Source: Lister, 1966, pp. 181–82; Almada, 1968, p. 523.

CORRALITOS AND MINAS DE SAN PEDRO, CHIHUAHUA

1. Edwin Denison Morgan was born at Throgs Neck, New York, on October 19, 1854. He was named Alfred Waterman at birth but after the death of his father was renamed Edwin Denison after his grandfather. Between 1873 and 1877 he attended Harvard where he was champion heavyweight boxer. Sports played an important part in his life, so much so that he became a member of the Westchester Polo Team, master of hounds at the Meadowbrook Club, director of the National Horse Show Association, and a member of the New York State Racing Commission for ten years. His yachting activities led him to be managing director of the *Columbia* in the America's Cup competition, and with his schooner *Wanderer* and his steam yacht *Amy* he cruised the world.

   Morgan, upon graduation from Harvard, joined his grandfather's mercantile, banking, and brokerage business in New York City, becoming cotrustee of the Car Trust of New York and of the New York and Pacific Car Trust. He was also closely associated with the Metropolitan Trust Company of New York and the Phillipsburg (New Jersey) Coal and Land Company. Between 1899 and 1916 Morgan was president of both the Corralitos Cattle Company and the Candelaria Mining Company. Periodically he inspected the ranch and when he did so, he traveled on a special train, presumably in his own car. In August 1914, on one such trip, he took with him E. C. Houghton, who managed the Corralitos ranch after Britton Davis resigned. E. D. Morgan died on June 12, 1933.

   Source: *National Cyclopaedia*, vol. 44, p. 350; El Paso *Herald*, August 26, 1914.

2. This ranch, 115 miles southwest of Juárez, was purchased in 1880 by William Wallace, Sr. Shortly thereafter, Maj. George B. Zimpleman of Austin and Judge J. F. Crosby of Houston obtained title to it and interested E. D. Morgan and his financial group in it. With home offices at Juárez until 1901 and

afterward in El Paso, Britton Davis served as general manager until 1906. Later E. C. Houghton was general manager. The land of the Corralitos Cattle Company fed their cattle and at the same time offered prime mining opportunities; thus the Candelaria Mining Company was formed and a concentrator built at Juárez. To coordinate these varied activities, the company built its own railroad from Juárez to Casas Grandes, 147 miles in length, without issuing a bond.

The company prospered until 1916, when constant raids forced the suspension of activities. At its height the ranch and mines supported approximately six thousand persons, one hundred of whom were Americans. Even with the interference of the revolutionary activities, the ranch still had 60,000 head of cattle in 1924. Dry-land farming produced wheat, corn, fruit and vegetables.

In 1941 the ranch was sold by Richard Trimble of New York and E. C. Houghton, the ranch manager, to Rodrigo M. Quevedo of Chihuahua and William W. Wallace of El Paso for $100,000. By then the ranch had lost its cattle as the multitudinous acres were lacking in activity.

Source: *Mexican World*, June 24, 1924, p. 7; El Paso *Times*, August 3, 1924.

3. Díaz served Mexico as president from May 1877, to May 1911, resigning when the Madero revolution was in full swing. The encouragement given mining is reflected in the fact that gold production in 1877–78 totaled $1,473,912.32, while in 1907–08 it reached the sum of $40,572,185.20. Gold and silver production for 1908–09 amounted to $125,890,089.33. Railroad lines also were extended, growing from 578 kilometers in 1877 to 24,160 in 1909.

Source: Godoy, 1910, pp. 114–15, 117; Hanay, 1917, pp. 1ff.

4. This was the famous Babícora Ranch purchased in 1887 by Sen. George Hearst just as Geronimo, the Apache chief, was captured. Hearst purchased 200,000 acres, but the reported

price varies between twenty and forty cents per acre. Later, the ranch grew to 900,000 acres, or 1400 square miles, and ownership passed to Senator Hearst's son, William Randolph Hearst. The younger Hearst borrowed so heavily against the ranch that his mother, Phoebe, held a mortgage on it, but even so Hearst continued to manage it. The 48,000 head of cattle on it were controlled by an army of 150 vaqueros.

In 1903 Hearst married and took his bride to visit the ranch. Jack Follansbee served as general manager until about 1905 when he was succeeded by John C. Hayes. In 1915, when Pancho Villa's irregular army raided Babícora, Hayes fled to El Paso, leaving Maximiliano Marquez in charge. Three times in 1915 and 1916 Villa raided Hearst property stealing cattle and killing at least one American employee. Finally Gen. John J. Pershing's forces chased Villa across Hearst land in 1916.

By 1921 the ranch was still intact but its condition was bad. War had taken its toll. In 1925 Hearst wanted to restock and he sent a correspondent, Frazier Hunt, to inspect the property and do a series of articles on the Mexican government. Hunt called this a "gumshoe job" because one of his goals was to persuade the government to eject some persons who had encroached on Babícora property.

The Babícora stayed in Hearst's hands until 1943 when it was sold back to the Mexican government for $2,500,000.

Source: *National Cyclopaedia*, vol. 1, p. 315; Carson and Bates, 1936, pp. 13–14; Lister, 1966, pp. 253, 279; Swanberg, 1961, pp. 34, 190, 206–7; Lundberg, 1937, pp. 19, 220–21, 333; Hunt, 1938, pp. 293–94; El Paso *Herald*, April 4, 1941; El Paso *Times*, June 1, 1956.

5. Beresford's story is best told by Porter, 1970.

6. The Boyd ranch was named La Carreta. How it was acquired, its size, and the date of acquisition by the Boyd family have not been established; however Alfred O. Boyd published his description of life on the La Carreta in *Frontier Times* (February–March, 1963), pp. 34–35, 44.

7. This ranch was controlled by the Palomas Land and Cattle Company. It stretched for a distance of 70 miles in northern Chihuahua along the New Mexico border. The ranch was in the bleached Chihuahua desert at a spot as uninviting to humanity as any place in the state, and it supported a huge cattle operation. On March 8, 1916, Pancho Villa crossed Palomas land to attack the United States at Columbus, New Mexico. A few days before that Villa had attacked a group of Palomas cowboys, relieving them of their hundred head of cattle and sixty horses. Juan Favala was one of the group that survived.

   By 1940 the ranch, said to be valued at $5 million, had Marshall Stephenson of Columbus, New Mexico, as a principal owner; however, Juárez labor unions agitated for its return to the government. That year it was confiscated to remove the Americans, and the Palomas Land and Cattle Company ceased to exist.

   Source: El Paso *Times*, January 27, 1941, and May 20, 1956; Lister, 1966, pp. 242–48.

8. Edward Cone Houghton became ranch manager of the Corralitos Company in 1895. He was born in Santa Fe, New Mexico, on November 6, 1861, the son of Jacob and Ann Caroline Shoemaker Houghton. Educated at St. Michael's College in Santa Fe, he ranched in northwest Texas and the Black Range in New Mexico before joining the Corralitos Company. He was employed by the ranch for the remainder of his life, but he left Mexico during the troublesome times of the Mexican Revolution which began in 1911. In 1917 Houghton was residing in Las Cruces, New Mexico, but by 1928, he again lived in El Paso, where he died on April 10.

   Houghton was a member of El Paso Masonic Lodge No. 130, A.F. & A.M., the Scottish Rite, the Shrine, and the York Rite. He belonged to the Episcopal Church.

   Source: El Paso *Times*, April 11, 1928; El Paso *Herald*, April 10, 1928, and April 13, 1928; Twitchell, 1917, vol. 3, p. 219.

9. This was the Los Ojitos Ranch which Beresford purchased in 1884. At that time it consisted of 4000 acres, but by the time of his death in 1906 it had 160,000 acres and was well stocked.
   Source: Porter, 1970, p. 18.

10. Adm. Lord Charles Beresford entered the British navy in 1859 at the age of fourteen, rising through the ranks to become commander of Britain's Mediterranean Fleet from 1905 to 1907, and of the Channel Fleet from 1907 to 1909. He retired from the navy in 1911. Books he wrote included *The Life of Nelson and His Times, The Break-Up of China, The Betrayed,* and *Memories.* When his brother, Lord Delaval Beresford died in 1906, Sir Charles visited El Paso to settle the estate. Since the presence of the Lord Admiral of the British Navy in El Paso created quite a stir, Parker naturally remembered him.
    Source: Porter, 1970, p. 13.

11. Florida J. Wolfe, a Negro, was born in Illinois in either 1867 or 1871. She met Lord Beresford in Chihuahua City and they "formed a mutual liking for one another." At his insistence she gave up her job as a nurse in the home of the American Consul in Chihuahua and went to live with Lord Beresford. Lady Flo was a good rancher and handled the affairs of Beresford so successfully that even though the two were not married, his estate had to settle with her. After Beresford's death, Lady Flo moved to El Paso where she died on May 19, 1913.
    Source: Porter, 1970, pp. 10, 12, 30.

12. Delaval Beresford died at Enderlin, North Dakota, on the night of December 23, 1906. Enderlin is almost 800 miles northwest of Chicago.
    Source: Porter, 1970, pp. 3–5.

13. Even though Parker makes a distinction, Minas de San Pedro has come to be known by historians as Corralitos, after the company that owned it. It was founded in 1839 by two older

men, D. Angel and D. Mariame Aguirre. In 1847 or 1848 it became the seat of government for the district of Galeana, and with the advent of the influx of American capital it grew to large proportions. In addition to the Corralitos Land and Cattle Company office there, the Candelaria Mining Company officed 4 miles north at Candelaria. There the Candelaria Company had stores, hotels, and residences for its employees. Its main mines were the León, the Congreso, the San Celestino, the San Fernando, the Candelaria, and the Corralitos. In addition, numerous other mines were leased out to other operators. Thus the term "Minas de San Pedro" referred to Corralitos, Candelaria, and the mines nearby in the district of Galeana. In 1907, population at Minas de San Pedro, including the Candelaria, Corralitos, and León mines was 2235.

Source: Almada, 1968, pp. 119, 336; Griggs, 1907, pp. 182, 192–93, 294–95; Sierra Madre Railway District (Mining File Folder 606–40).

14. On May 4, 1896, the Mexican government authorized the building of the line between Ciudad Juárez and Corralitos, a distance of 115 miles. This standard gauge line, owned by the Río Grande, Sierra Madre and Pacific Railway Company, was popularly known as the Corralitos Railway. Service was opened to Corralitos in May 1897 and to Casas Grandes in August of the same year. In 1908 William C. Greene, the copper magnate, served as president of the executive committee, and on October 26, 1909, it became part of the Mexico Northwestern Railway property. Ore from the mines of the Corralitos Company and cattle from the big ranch provided much of the traffic for the railroad. Three dollars per ton was the going rate for delivery of the ore from Minas de San Pedro to Juárez in 1908.

Source: *Mexican Yearbook*, 1908, pp. 390–91; Hoard, Mexican Northwestern Railway Company, p. 7; Sutton, 1908 (typescript); Almada, 1968, p. 206.

15. Lake Guzmán, fed by the Casas Grandes River, is in the Judicial District of Galeana. Its area is approximately 56 square miles. In Spanish times it was known as "Laguna de la Ascensión."

      Source: Almada, 1968, p. 247.

16. A stope is an excavation from which the ore was extracted either above or below a level in a series of steps.

      Source: Sonnichsen, 1971, p. 144.

17. The adit is an almost horizontal entrance to a mine.

      Source: Fay, 1947, p. 4.

18. David Bruce Smith was born in Dundee, Forfarshire, Scotland, in 1867 or 1868, and he died in Los Angeles, California, on September 27, 1927. By profession he was a mining superintendent and, in addition to being connected with the Candelaria Company, he was with the Ahumada Lead Company of Santa Eulalia, Chihuahua. He died of an infection contracted while he was inspecting mining properties in Mexico. Smith belonged to several El Paso social and fraternal organizations including the El Paso Country Club, Lodge 187 of the Order of the Elks, El Paso Lodge No. 130, A. F. & A. M., and El Maida Shrine Temple. He was buried in Evergreen Cemetery, El Paso, on October 1, 1927.

      Source: El Paso *Times*, September 28, 1927, and September 29, 1927, and October 1, 1927; St. Clement Church Register, book 4, p. 38.

19. An ASARCO smelter in Zacatecas has proved impossible to locate. Parker is referring to the year 1898 as the time he met D. Bruce Smith. ASARCO was not formed until the following year, 1899, even though the Guggenheims had been in Mexico since 1892. They had smelters at Monterrey and Aguascalientes, but only an ore-buying agency in Zacatecas by 1898. Smith may have worked in one of those.

      Source: Marcosson, 1949, p. 19; Bernstein, 1964, p. 38.

20. A winze is an opening connecting a level in a mine with another level below.

    Source: Sonnichsen, 1971, p. 144.

21. The Congreso-León mines were originally two separate mines, but extensive exploration resulted in underground connections between the two. Eventually these two mines and the San Celestino were grouped under the title "León." In 1904, just six years after Parker first went there, production from the Congreso y León was 161 metric tons. The revolution changed things and by 1935 J. H. Blackwell owned the mines. Ten years later, in 1945, he sold them to the Minas de Durango company.

    Source: Griggs, 1907, p. 192; Sierra Madre Railway District (Mining File Folder 606–40); *Engineering and Mining Journal*, October, 1945, pp. 144, 146.

22. Sulphides are primary ores, in this case compounds of bivalent sulphur with lead, gold, and silver, while carbonates are formed by combining a chemical agent with carbon dioxide. Carbonates of metals are often found in the upper portions of the ore bodies and as a consequence different enrichments in the concentrating processes are required for sulphides and carbonates.

    Source: Joralemon, 1973, p. 397; Dana, 1920, pp. 33–108, 261–309.

23. This organization belonged part and parcel to the Corralitos Land and Cattle Company. Its home offices were in Juárez until 1901 when they were moved to El Paso. E. D. Morgan was chairman of the board, Britton Davis was managing director, and Edmond de Goncer was resident director. De Goncer served until 1909. The Candelaria Company sold its output to the Juárez Company, also owned by the Corralitos firm, which in turn marketed the ore with the Guggenheim Com-

pany at Juárez. From there, the ore was distributed to smelters at Monterrey, Aguascalientes, El Paso and Pueblo, Colorado. The company owned all of the mines at Minas de San Pedro and Candelaria, but it leased some of them to individuals. In 1905 the Candelaria Company produced 9354 metric tons of ore valued at $237,000.

Source: Griggs, 1907, p. 101; Sierra Madre Railway District (Mining File Folder 606–40); "Geronimo's Maddest Outrage," page unknown; Weed and Probert, Report on the Candelaria Mining Property (typescript).

24. The process described here deals with the lead content which was necessary in the smelting process. These carbonates were apparently of the rich self-fluxing type because of their lead content. Generally, sulphides are noted for their "dryness" (low lead content in relation to silver) and carbonates are noted for their "wetness." Parker apparently found a happy medium.

Source: Bernstein, 1964, pp. 22, 33–34.

25. The source of the Chinese entry into Mexico is uncertain. One theory is that they migrated southward from the gold and silver mines of California, Arizona, and New Mexico, following the line of least resistance and the least prejudice. Another factor was the Chinese Exclusion Act passed by the United States Congress in 1882. It deterred the Chinese from entering the United States for a period of twenty years. As a result many Chinese migrated to Mexico with the hope that later they could make their way into the United States. Those who remained in Mexico are said to have made excellent citizens and in time were amalgamated with the Mexican population. By 1900 2837 Chinese were reported living in Mexico, a figure that increased to over 40,000 by 1920.

Source: Coolidge, 1909, pp. 168–82; Callicott, 1931, p. 308; Martin, 1907, vol. 2, p. 209; *Mexican Yearbook*, 1908, p. 12; Tays, 1907, pp. 622–23.

LIFE AT MINAS DE SAN PEDRO

1. Parker married Olive Genevieve McCourt at White Oaks on November 29, 1893. Her mother was then married to William C. McDonald who later became governor of the state of New Mexico. The Parkers' children were named Lina, Frances, Genevieve, Margaret, and Morris Jr. Mrs. Parker died in 1955.

   Source: Leonard, 1922, p. 1965; Sonnichsen, 1971, pp. 84–85.

2. Richard Franklin Stovall was born in Kaufman, Texas, on October 7, 1864, the son of Richard Lewis and Sarah Tankersley Stovall. He graduated from the medical department of the University of Louisville, Kentucky, in 1884, and for the next ten years lived in Deming, New Mexico, serving as surgeon for the Santa Fe and Southern Pacific railways. While there he was elected in 1892 to a term in the New Mexico Territorial Legislature. By 1896 he was living in California, but he soon moved to Minas de San Pedro where Parker knew him. Afterward, Stovall took charge of the Mimbres Hot Springs Health Resort in Grant County and entered a homestead adjacent to it, where he began ranching. He was still living in 1925.

   Source: Coan, 1925, vol. 3, pp. 118–19.

3. This marriage occurred on September 2, 1899, in St. Clement Episcopal Church in El Paso. The Reverend Cabell Martin performed the ceremony.

   Source: St. Clement Register, book 2, p. 216.

4. Colonia Dublan was founded in 1888 and flourished magnificently until the revolution. Its story is outlined in Romney, 1938, pp. 95–101.

5. Don Miguel Ahumada was born in Colima on September 29, 1844, and he died at El Paso, Texas, on August 27, 1916. Elected governor of Chihuahua on October 4, 1892, he served until 1904.

   Source: Almada, 1968, pp. 21–22.

6. The source of the Santa María River is in the Sierra de Choreachic in the Municipio de Namiquipa, at a place named Las Chepas. Mountain ranges on the east of the river include the San José, Piloncillos, Tunas, and Tecolote, while on the west are the La Culebra, Anco San Joaquín, Santa Catarina, La Escondida, and El Cristo. The river flows from south to north for 200 miles until it empties into Laguna de Santa María.

    Source: Colaca, 1955, pp. 33–35; *Atlas Geográfico*, 1966, p. 7.

7. The Rurales were first proposed in 1855 owing to the thefts that were taking place on the public roads. José M. Lafragua, minister of government, proposed that the state governors create the frontier police but the act was not accomplished until 1861 when President Benito Juárez issued the order. Thereafter, through the reign of Porfirio Díaz, they were quite effective and ruthless in enforcing their particular brand of law. Under Díaz, who controlled through his governors, the Rurales received good pay, spirited horses, and flashy uniforms. Traveling in small groups, they attained great pride in running a crime-free district. When Gov. Miguel Ahumada organized the Rurales in Chihuahua in 1895, he gave authority for them to shoot anyone attempting escape. This was the order that led to the famed *ley de fuga* because most of the prisoners were shot as they tried to get away. The justice of the matter might be questioned, but not its effectiveness. Crime dropped to almost nothing.

    Source: *Diccionario Porrúa*, 1970, vol. 2, pp. 1821–22; Lister, 1966, p. 170.

HACIENDA DURAZO, SONORA

1. Moctezuma, the headquarters of the Municipio of Moctezuma, is located on the west slope of the Sierra Madre south of Douglas, Arizona, and 90 miles northeast of Hermosillo, the

capital of Sonora. Originally founded in 1644 by the Jesuit missionary, Marcos del Río, the villa was named San Miguel Arcángel de Oposura. Gradually, the name shortened to Oposura, and on September 9, 1828, the legislature of the State of Occidente (now Sonora) changed it to the present Moctezuma. It is situated on the Moctezuma River in the heart of territory occupied by Yaqui and Mayo Indians. Mining is its chief economic endeavor but in the area are many haciendas and ranchos where cattle and grain are produced. Also, the region furnishes a certain kind of rock which when polished resembles fine marble. Population was approximately 2100 persons in 1968.

Source: Dunbier, 1968, p. 152; *Diccionario Porrúa*, 1971, vol. 2, p. 1370; Pfefferkorn, 1949, pp. 80, 245; Almada, 1952, p. 481; Roca, 1967, p. 20.

2. This town of Lampazos, District of Moctezuma, State of Sonora, has all but disappeared from Mexican history. Probably it is a mining ghost town; none of the histories or reference works on Sonora mentions its existence. An article in 1910 made mention of a silver mine at Lampazos "in the south of the Moctezuma district" which had been productive for many years. The following year the mine was credited with having shipped thirty-four pounds of silver bullion. Don Miguel A. López was the leading miner and Francisco Gallego was a cattle raiser, farmer, and merchant. Located south and east of the community of Moctezuma (but the maps are not to scale so they do not reveal the distance), Lampazos seems to have gone into oblivion along with others of its like.

Source: Merrill, 1910, p. 157; Coll, 1911, p. 14; *Map of Moctezuma District*; García y Alva, 1905–07, unpaged.

3. In 1878 the site of present Douglas, Arizona, was known as Black Water, a name used because of the dirty water hole that was there. The place was little used until 1901 when the town was established and named for James Stuart Douglas, who

was then a mining superintendent for the Phelps Dodge Corporation. Thus Parker was nearby the same year the town was begun. Conditions had to be primitive. Later development came as a result of the railroad Phelps Dodge built from Bisbee to Douglas to Nacozari in Sonora, and from the smelter the company placed at Douglas.

Source: Granger, 1960, p. 36; Cleland, 1952, pp. 143–44.

4. Agua Prieta (Spanish for Black Water) is the seat of government for the judicial district of Agua Prieta. Located adjacent to Douglas, Arizona, the town had a population of 10,479 in 1940. The entire district counted only 13,124 persons that year. This Mexican town was given its name in 1855 by Colonel William H. Emory to verify the recognition of the boundary limits between Mexico and the United States according to the Treaty of La Mesilla. It was an insignificant place until 1901 when the Phelps Dodge Corporation built a railroad from Douglas to their rich mine at Nacozari. Thereafter Agua Prieta thrived as the port of exit for the metal leaving Mexico to be processed at Douglas and other smelters.

Agua Prieta served as the site of two notable battles during the Mexican Revolution. On April 13, 1911, revolutionary forces led by Santiago Chambers, Antonio Rojas, and Antonio López were defeated by the federalists Captain José Vargas and Colonel Reinaldo Díaz. When Pancho Villa attacked the town on October 31, 1915, he was repulsed by General Plutarco Elias Calles who was assisted by American artillery.

Source: Almada, 1952, p. 18.

5. This passage is through the valley of the Río Grande de Santiago, whose waters shed both upon Guadalajara, in the state of Jalisco, and Tepic in the state of Nayarit. Guadalajara is approximately 120 miles southeast of Tepic.

Source: *Atlas Geográfico*, 1966, p. 17.

6. The center of the Fronteras Valley is a large depression known locally as the valley of Turicachi. It is formed on the south by the Los Ajos mountains as they range to the Cananea, Purica,

La Ceniza, and Nainivacachi mountains, and to the west toward the Las Mesteñas, Santa Rosa, Las Grullas and El Potrero. The northern cordillera serves to part the waters of the Gila and Yaqui rivers. Agriculture is significant in the valley, but the population is small, being only 4179 persons in 1940, even though it had been settled in the middle of the seventeenth century by missionaries of the Company of Jesus. Its first name was Santa Rosa de Corodehuachi but that was later changed to El Presidio de las Fronteras de los Apaches and finally simply to Fronteras. Along the ribs of the arroyos, large ranches are to be found, and these comprise the major economic significance of the entire valley.

Source: Almada, 1952, pp. 281–82; Roca, 1967, pp. 176–85.

7. Morelos was founded at the junction of the Bavispe and Batepite rivers in 1898. It flourished until July 1912, when rebel troops commanded by Sanjinez camped in the streets, insulting the Mormons and destroying property. The conflict continued until the end of August when the colonists began retreating to the United States. As the Mormons moved out, additional Mexicans poured in to complete the devastation. Colonia Morelos was leveled by the end of September 1912.

Source: Romney, 1938, pp. 120–27, 193–200.

8. Gavilán is located on the Río Sonora between Ures and Hermosillo in the Judicial District of Ures. The mines there were discovered in 1764 but the settlement was never large. Parker found it primitive in 1901, and Paul Roca found it just as primitive half a century later.

Source: Roca, 1967, p. 171; Almada, 1952, p. 307.

9. Ignaz Pfefferkorn, another observer, wrote: "In Sonora everything crawls with spiders." The arachnids Parker describes belong to the order *Phalangida*, but popularly they are called daddy long-legs, grandfather-greybeards, and harvestmen or harvesters.

Source: Comstock, 1913, pp. 53–58; Pfefferkorn, 1949, pp. 131–32.

10. The Southern Pacific Railroad of Mexico had completed its line from Hermosillo, the capital of the state of Sonora, to Nogales in October 1882, but that line was substantially to the west of Parker's interests at El Gavilán. Talk of completing the railroad might have been around when Parker was there in 1901. A proposed railroad from Baviscora to Cananea shows on maps as late as 1908.

    The reality of the situation was that the Phelps Dodge Corporation had acquired the Nacozari mine in 1895 from the Guggenheim interests, and that they also acquired the Copper Queen mine at Bisbee. Between these two mines they established their new smelter at Douglas in 1901 and then commenced a railroad to run south 75 miles to the Nacozari mines. The line was begun in 1901, the year of Parker's visit, and completed in 1904. Incorporated under Mexican law, this road was named the Nacozari Railroad. That is as close as the railroad came to El Gavilán in Parker's active years.

    Source: Cleland, 1952, pp. 131–35, 143; Almada, 1952, pp. 275–78; *Mexican Mining Journal*, February 1908, p. 17.

11. Don Venanzio Durazo has remained obscure in the literature of Sonora. The only certain mention of him concerns his move to Douglas, Arizona, in February 1911, and even then the newspaper merely stated that he rented a house for twenty-five members of his immediate family. It was to be a temporary asylum for the duration of the revolution. Francisco Durazo enthusiastically embraced the Madero cause in 1910. Later, one Rafael Durazo became a major in P. Elias Calles's army.

    Source: Rivera, 1969, pp. 168, 335, 454; Pace, 1974, p. 13; *Mexican Mining Journal*, June 1909, p. 30.

12. By 1898 Tom Davenport was living in El Paso where he worked as a fireman on the Southern Pacific Railroad. He remained until sometime in 1899, when he moved from El

Paso, apparently to Minas de San Pedro. In 1906 he lived in Cumpas, Sonora, where he was part owner with Morris Parker of the La Recuerda Mine. James Parker sold the mine in June 1906, to Charles A. Romadka of the El Globo Mining and Milling Company.

Source: *Evans and Worley's Directory*, 1898, p. 122; James Parker to Thomas L. Davenport, June 14, 1906; C. A. Romadka to James Parker, June 25, 1906; James Parker to Charles A. Romadka, August 8, 1906 (Mss. in Mining File-Mexico, Folder 53).

13. These were probably jaguar, which are often called the Mexican Tiger and the American Tiger. Other more remote possibilities are that they were margay, ocelot, bobcat, or even cougar.

Source: Seton, 1953, vol. 1, pt. 1, pp. 3–34.

14. Born in Hermosillo in 1859, Francisco H. García graduated from the military college at Chapultepec in 1878, and thereafter followed a military career. In addition to numerous assignments in Mexico, he served with military attachés in Washington and London. In May 1890, he was promoted to lieutenant colonel, and in September 1904, he became a colonel. His retirement was in 1911, but he reentered the army in 1913 and under President Huerta became governor of the state of Sonora as well as brigadier general of the army. During the revolution, when the Federal army dissolved, García escaped to the United States.

Source: Almada, 1952, pp. 298–99.

15. Without doubt, the best treatment on the subject of haciendas is McBride, 1971, pp. 25–81. Another recommended survey is Whetten, 1948, pp. 90–107. In the latter part of the nineteenth century when American capitalists invaded Mexico, the hacienda was one of the institutions which captured their imagination. Typical accounts of these are Kirkham, 1909, pp. 110–12;

and Winter, 1907, pp. 27–30. For critical views of the system see Flippin, 1889, pp. 184–89, and Katz, 1974, pp. 1–47.

In depth studies are scarce. As late as 1969, Ward Barrett was noting "the lack of published information concerning Spanish colonial plantations." In this case he did something about it by writing *The Sugar Hacienda of the Marqueses Del Valle*. Another study is Lamb, 1908, pp. 663–64.

16. Variously Guasabas, Huásabas was founded in 1651 by Marcos del Río, missionary for the Opata nation of the Lower Pima Indians. He named it San Francisco Javier de Guasabas. During colonial times this settlement was famous for its missionaries, having been headquarters for Juan Nentvig and Joseph Och. By 1940 the pueblo had 1314 inhabitants.

Source: Almada, 1952, pp. 349–50; Roca, 1967, pp. 216–21; Treutlein, 1965, pp. xiii–xv; Pfefferkorn, 1949, pp. 254–65.

17. While the history of Huásabas is available in some detail, the story of Granados is rather unknown. It is on the Bavispe River about 30 miles south of Huásabas and 115 miles northeast of Hermosillo. The principal source of income is from grain and livestock, and its population in 1940 was 1124. About one-third of its people could neither read nor write at that time.

Source: Almada, 1952, p. 318; Roca, 1967, pp. 206, 218, 222.

18. Gramophone is a brand name for phonograph. Emile Berliner started manufacturing the Gramophone in 1894, but Eldridge R. Johnson of Camden, New Jersey, made substantial improvements. By June 1897, the Improved Gramophone was being produced and advertised into immortality. The model Parker heard in the wilds of Sonora is doubtless the same one shown in the picture where the chubby black and white fox terrier peers into the horn and listens to "His Master's Voice."

Source: Gelatt, 1955, pp. 83–91.

PILARES DE NACOZARI, SONORA

1. James Stuart Douglas, Jr., was born in Megantic Township, Quebec, Canada, on June 19, 1868. He was educated at Phoenixville, Pennsylvania, Toronto, Canada, and New York before he moved to Arizona in 1889. He liked farming, but the interests of his father soon lured him into mining. At the time Parker knew him he managed both the Moctezuma Copper Company and the Picacho Mine, both subsidiaries of Phelps Dodge. In 1913 he managed the Cananea Consolidated Copper Company at Cananea before he put together the United Verde Extension Mining Company, a corporation he served as president until 1938. He served the American Red Cross in France in 1917, where he became friends with the French Premier George Clemenceau. Douglas became a United States citizen in 1869, and was active in the politics of the Democratic Party until 1938, when he returned to Canada to reassume his Canadian citizenship. He died at Montreal on January 2, 1949.

    Source: *National Cyclopaedia*, 1967, vol. 38, p. 165.

2. When James Stuart Douglas died on June 25, 1918, the editor who penned his obituary for the *Engineering and Mining Journal* (July 6, 1918), pp. 18–20, predicted: "Some biographer will write a great book about Doctor Douglas." As of 1979, that prediction had not come to pass. Douglas' name is spread throughout the annals of mining magazines, but no one has told his story. The most extensive source on him is Langton, 1940.

    Douglas was born at Quebec, Canada, on November 4, 1837. He studied medicine in Canada, Germany and Scotland and later was a student of theology at the University of Edinburgh. And from medicine and theology he turned to mining because his father had an interest in it. Douglas was forty-three years of age when he became interested in the Copper

Queen mine at Bisbee, Arizona, and he, in turn, persuaded the partners of Phelps Dodge and Company to invest in the mine. He took his fee in shares and became a partner. Thereafter he managed the mining interests until his retirement in 1917. He wrote and published profusely, received many honors, and was from *all* accounts highly respected when he died at Spuyten Duyvil near Quebec. One of his books, which tells much about his father and his family background and early education, is *Journals and Reminiscences of James Douglas, M.D.* (New York: Privately Printed, 1910).

3. Lewis Williams Douglas was born at Bisbee on July 2, 1894. Educated at Amherst College and the Massachusetts Institute of Technology, he returned to Arizona in 1921. In 1923 his election to the Arizona House of Representatives heralded his entry into politics. Thereafter, he served in the 70th–73d Congresses of the United States as congressman-at-large from Arizona. On March 7, 1933, President Franklin D. Roosevelt appointed him as Director of the Budget with the objective of making it balance.

   In May 1933, as the president held a news conference, reporter Arthur Krock was there to note the presence of Lewis Douglas. He wrote:

   > Once or twice he [Douglas] was called upon by the President for precise information, which he gave in the quiet, modest manner that is part of his fine grain. That manner, and the personality which it in part expresses has had a great deal to do with Mr. Douglas's attainment of great public stature. He might well have been able, upright and courageous as he is, but he owes much of his success to unusual personal charm. The sum of these qualities has made this 38 year old Arizonian the real head of the Roosevelt cabinet.

   By June 1933, some talk in Washington stated that Douglas would become the secretary of treasury, but it did not happen. Even so, the debates in the Senate between Senators Huey

P. Long of Louisiana (anti-Douglas) and Henry Fountain Ashurst of Arizona (pro-Douglas) are amusing as well as informative. As political tides shifted, Douglas and Roosevelt came to have more disagreements on monetary policy until Douglas resigned in September 1934. It was the "end of a period of highly distinguished, loyal and belligerently honest service" which received not "a public word of thanks from the President."

Later, Douglas became president and chairman of the board of the Mutual Life Insurance Company of New York and from 1947–1950 was United States ambassador to the Court of St. James's. As with his ancestors, his honors are legion. In 1978 he listed addresses both in Tucson and New York.

Source: *Who's Who in America*, 1974, pp. 832–33; New York *Times*, February 24, 1933, p. 2, c.5, and March 7, 1933, p. 7, c.4, and May 19, 1933, p. 16, c.8, and September 29, 1934, p. 14, c.6, and October 27, 1934, p. 26, c.7; *Congressional Record*, 1933, pp. 4583–84, 4589.

4. H. B. Layton's contemporary description of the three-foot-gauge railroad stated that it was "as carefully constructed as any trunk line in the United States." The grades were compared to "some of the Colorado mountain climbers," and the road climbed more than 600 feet in its length. It had three trestles, one of which was 400 feet long and 81 feet high and it featured a 400-foot-long tunnel through solid rock. The account concluded:

> The 40-lb. rails are all laid on the tie plates and are aligned to a lead pencil point. During the period of construction 700 Mexicans have been employed at one time, with only J. W. D. Moodie, superintendent, his assistant, Mr. York, and one or two other skilled track men to direct such a motley army. The road is estimated to have cost $63,000 Mexican currency per mile.

Source: Layton, June 9, 1900, p. 679.

5. James Douglas, Jr., became assayer and timekeeper for the Commercial Mining Company in 1890, and for the larger part of the following decade he was superintendent of the Senator, Copper Basin, and Big Bug mines owned by Commercial; thus the sale just prior to Parker's arrival.

   Source: *National Cyclopaedia*, vol. 38, p. 165.

6. American Smelting and Refining Company owned by the Guggenheims of New York acquired this mine in 1890 from Colonel John Wein. For seven years the Guggenheims ran a burro train operation owing to their inadequate equipment. Finally, Louis D. Ricketts recommended that Phelps Dodge purchase it, which they did in 1897.

   Source: Bernstein, 1965, pp. 59–60; Layton, June 9, 1900, pp. 678–79, and June 16, 1900, p. 707; Leland, 1930, pp. 1–3.

7. For a thumbnail history of the El Paso and Southwestern Railroad see Myrick, 1970, pp. 82–94. Many of the manuscripts associated with the railroad are in the Southern Pacific Collection, Archives, University of Texas at El Paso. These cover the years 1905–1924.

8. Difficulty is encountered in determining exactly which Yaqui revolt Parker is discussing. By their own admission, these Indians had been in constant rebellion since 1825. In 1904 Mexican soldiers fought with "Yaqui workers" and as a result many of the Yaquis were killed while others were sent to distant points. There was peace for a time in 1909, but in 1910 the fighting started again. Intermittent struggles continued on until 1927, when some of the Yaquis started moving north into Arizona and other parts of the United States.

   Source: Holden, 1936, pp. 129–31; Hu-Dehart, 1974, pp. 72–93.

9. By 1902 the Baldwin Locomotive Works of Pennsylvania had completed and sold 20,000 locomotives and they were scattered throughout the world. One of the machines located at

Nacozari was named "The General," but it cannot be ascertained that García was using it the day of the explosion.

Source: Kelly, 1946, pp. 1–5; *Engineering and Mining Journal*, June 9, 1900, p. 706, and November 3, 1900, pp. 513, 527, and December 29, 1900, p. 766; *History of the Baldwin Locomotive Works*, 1907, p. 92.

10. Jesús García was born on December 2, 1881, in Hermosillo, son of Don Francisco García and Doña Rosa Corona de García. The accident described by Parker took place on November 7, 1907, at 2 P.M. A statue was also erected to García near Francisco I. Madero Park in Hermosillo.

Source: "A Man Who Died . . . ," 1909, p. 29.

11. Some accounts state that a young American boy was a stowaway on the train and that "a few Mexicans" who were in a section house nearby were also blown to bits.

Source: "A Man Who Died . . . ," 1909, p. 29.

12. When James S. Douglas, Jr., gave up the management of the Phelps Dodge properties in Sonora in 1909, he was succeeded by J. S. Williams, Jr.

Source: *Mexican Mining Journal*, June 1909, p. 28.

LA REPUBLICA MINE, CHIHUAHUA

1. La República Mine was opened in 1894 by a native of Miñaca, Manuel Armado, who later sold it to Gibbs, White and Alexander. Parker bought it in June 1906 for $250,000.

La República Mining Company was chartered in New Mexico but its offices were in El Paso, with officers as follows: J. J. Mundy, president; W. E. Porter, vice-president; B. F. Darbyshire, secretary; and Morris B. Parker, treasurer and general manager. The company capitalized at one million shares, at a par value of $1.00 per share, some of which was sold in Kansas City, Missouri. When additional expansion came late in 1908, Parker turned the job of consulting engineer over to J. Gordon Hardy who lived on the property until it closed. In spite of the water problem in the mine, operations were profitable until revolutionary activities forced closure in 1913.

Source: García y Alva, 1905–07, unpaged; Parker, 1908, p. 12; *Mining and Scientific Press*, July 27, 1907, p. 107, and August 8, 1908, p. 188; Rogers, 1908, p. 682; *Mining World*: September 15, 1906, p. 324; July 31, 1909, p. 302; August 14, 1909, p. 394; *Mexican Mining Journal*: December 1907, p. 30; March 1908, p. 29; May 1908, p. 30; June 1908, p. 21; July 1908, p. 31; July 1910, p. 35; October 1910, p. 35; January 1911, p. 35; October 1911, p. 39; March 1912, p. 44; June 1912, p. 47; September 1912, p. 46.

2. In 1907 this mine was owned by the Chihuahua Copper Company with home offices in Lowell, Massachusetts. Morris Parker was manager of the firm which also owned the Buena Vista Mine. Both mines were located 20 miles west of Moctezuma, Chihuahua, at Sierra de los Arrados, District Bravos.

Source: Griggs, 1911, p. 327.

3. Thomas and William Dale operated this bank but additional information is scarce. They also had mining interests in the corporations of McDonald, Dale & Anderson, American Mining and Smelting Company, and the Mexican Gold Dredging Corporation.

Source: Griggs, 1911, pp. 340–41.

4. Founded by the Jesuits in 1680, Tomochi had 869 inhabitants in 1950. Parker saw it as an Indian village, but it had a history of revolution prior to and after his visit there. Located in what one journalist called the Longitude of War, the Tomochi Rebellion began on November 30, 1891, when Cruz Chávez led his followers in an assault on the government offices. They were defeated but retreated to the mountains and eventually

returned to harass the government troops that had been brought in from Guerrero and Pinos Altos.

Revolutionaries from Moris, Pinos Altos, Ocampo and Temósachic, collectively known as Tomochis, were defeated and executed in January 1892, but it did not end the revolutionary activities in the vicinity. Tomochis distinguished themselves in the revolution that began in 1910. The village's population consisted of thirty or so poor families in 1892 and it had not changed much when Parker was there in 1906.

Source: Lister, 1966, pp. 183–85, 215, 260; Almada, 1958, pp. 530–33.

5. The old mine at Ocampo is the Santa Juliana which has a misty, traditional history. Parker's statement that this mine has been in continuous operation for two centuries cannot be proven, but there is evidence stating that it was worked prior to 1810 when the district was abandoned and the mines left to fill up with water. In 1818 José de Herrero opened the El Refugio del Rosario and other mines soon developed. The community in the center of the mines was named Jesús María by its founders, Tomás Bon, José Tomás de Riveras, and Vicente Pancorbo. By 1821 there were over two hundred claims up and down the canyon and the region has prospered since. Famous mines include the Candelaria, Nuestra Señora Del Rayón, Santa Margarita, Rosario, and San Rafael. By 1840 the Santa Juliana, the mine Parker mentions, was owned by John MacDonald, but by 1858 J. C. Henriquez operated it. Next it became the property of Matias Alzua and B. Phelps, but their operations were seriously hampered by raids from Apaches. Foreign investments came in 1886 with the Refugio Mining and Milling Company owned by men from Omaha and San Francisco, one of whom was John J. Waterson. In 1890 Waterson leased several mines and built a ten-stamp mill, later doubled, which he operated profitably until 1902, when he sold out to an English company. The Waterson mill

was the big one in operation at the time Parker first visited there. Jesús María became Ocampo sometime between 1883 and 1906, at which time it was the most populous town in western Chihuahua. The revolution changed that, and the town had 310 inhabitants in 1950. Its location is at the confluence of the La Cumbre and Santa Rita rivers.

Source: Almada, 1958, pp. 369–70; Dahlgren, 1883, pp. 126–28; Anderson, 1908, pp. 12–13; Linton, 1912, pp. 457–59; Hutchinson, 1906, pp. 418–20; Griggs, 1911, pp. 74–77, 347–49.

6. Concheño came into existence in 1889 when Juan Hernández established the San Ciriaco mine. The property was developed by Compañía Beneficiadora del Concheño which built a 150-ton mill and cyanide plant. This organization sold to the Greene Gold-Silver Company which boomed the town in 1906 and 1907. Then came the bust as described by Charles Anderson in 1908: ". . . Concheño today is a deserted village except for a few families of Mexicans who lead a hand to mouth existence . . . Concheño of today is vastly different from the Concheño of a year ago when the Greene Gold-Silver Co. was running and the camp was bustling with life and activity."

Source: Anderson, 1908, p. 11; Almada, 1958, p. 110; Griggs, 1911, pp. 306–7.

7. Pinos Altos abounds with *antiguas* (old mines from the Spanish era) which were taken over by an English company about 1875. Their main mine, the Santo Niño, was operated by John B. G. Hepburn and John Carr. Charles Anderson wrote that they were doing a thriving business — "Gold ore, 30 stamps running, doing well, extensive workings" — until January 6, 1883, when Hepburn was murdered by a "drunken lawless mob." The leaders of this mob were promptly shot. By 1907 the Negociación de Pinos Altos had control of 17,000 mining claims, including the Santo Niño, in a concession of 70 square miles of land. Their rights to the minerals lasted until 1918.

T. N. Barnsdale of Pittsburg and W. P. Dunham of Los Angeles were owners, E. M. Ray was manager, and B. M. Ray was superintendent. John B. Walton was the company prospector. The Pinos Altos company was famous for its hospitality, which lasted until the revolution forced closure. In 1950 Pino Altos had five mining claims and 169 persons.

Source: Dahlgren, 1883, pp. 140–41; Griggs, 1911, pp. 307, 348–49; Anderson, 1908, p. 12; Almada, 1968, p. 414.

8. This telephone line ran from La República to Sahuayacan to Ocampo, where a telegraph line connected the mines with the outside world at Miñaca, the nearest railway station. The distance from Miñaca to Sahuayacan was 125 miles. In 1905 Sahuayacan was a new development owned by the Sahuayacan Mining Company which headquartered at Ocampo and had John C. Treadwell as manager. By 1908 operations were suspended, but George Howard, the superintendent at Sahuayacan, expected activity by the beginning of 1909. The revolution killed development and there has been little done since.

Source: Treadwell, 1905, pp. 1213–16; Griggs, 1911, pp. 260–66; Anderson, 1908, p. 14.

9. Pascual Orozco was born February 10, 1882, and he was killed August 30, 1915. At maturity he was a tall lean man with blue eyes and a freckled complexion. Those who met him invariably mention the distrust that was obvious in his eyes. The best modern synthesis of his life and activities is Meyer, 1967.

10. I. J. Bush, a doctor with the Greene Gold-Silver Company, states in *Gringo Doctor*, pp. 226–31, that Villa at this time in his life was "just a pelado with a price on his head," and he tells the standard story of the evolution of Doroteo Arango, the arriero, into Pancho Villa, the revolutionary hero. Other, and varying accounts, are Schuster, 1947; Braddy, 1970; and Pinchon, 1933.

11. The testimony of Charles Anderson, who traveled this trail in 1908, corroborates Parker's statements. Anderson writes of the magnificent view before adding the negative aspect: "but as one looks away across the valleys and mountains to still loftier and steeper mountains and thinks of the days to be spent in scaling these and of nights when it is almost necessary to sleep sitting straddle of a tree to keep from sliding off the earth one can be excused from wanting to turn back and go around this country." Of the Cuchillo he wrote:

> Nobody ever rides up the Cuchillo much less down it! It is like going down a winding step ladder some thousands of feet and it is as rough and rocky and full of sharp sudden turns on the brink of the Hereafter as anything I ever want to experience ... There is nothing to be said of the descent of the Cuchillo. Those who have gone down it know. Those who have not, never can know until they go. We skidded and slid and slipped for hours down a zig-zag stretch about a foot wide, that zig-zagged about every 10 feet, into the river bed below.

Anderson made one more comment about the trail from Moris to the La República mine, for it was through the "highest, steepest mountains yet encountered." He concluded: "... we climbed up and up and up to the highest point of the highest mountain in sight over a steep slanting streak of a trail about 8 inches wide on an average and then jolted and bumped and stumbled down the other side, repeating the operation constantly from early morning until late in the afternoon, we arrived at La Republica mines only in a more or less intact condition." On the basis of such evidence, one comes to have a greater respect for the muleteers who hauled in the heavy equipment and for Parker himself, who is much calmer about it all than Anderson.

Source: Anderson, 1908, pp. 112–14.

12. Organized in 1902 to exploit "the most extensive and valuable [concessions] that have ever been granted to any company in

Mexico," the Greene Gold-Silver Company had exclusive rights to the mineral resources of 2,500,000 acres in Chihuahua. Clarence Chase was its manager and A. B. Fall its legal advisor. To serve his purposes, Greene bought a railroad, the Río Grande, Sierra Madre, and Pacific, which was extended to Temosachic, the company headquarters. In 1905 a 300-ton stamp mill began operation in Concheño and all things looked good. But the demise was already underway as Greene extended his finances too much. The corporation died on January 31, 1910, when Greene's exclusive rights to the minerals of the region expired.

Source: Sonnichsen, 1974, pp. 153–55, 209, 221, 226, 230–31.

13. This trip began at Temósachic on April 17, 1906, and the automobiles included two Pope-Toledos and two Panhards, but one of the Panhards remained in Temósachic. A reporter with the group thought the cars made noises "like a fat man out of breath" as they climbed the mountains and descended into the valleys. The night was spent at the Navidad mine. Next day brought a continuation, but the cars faltered as the last fifteen miles had to be done on muleback. Once at Ocampo the voyagers were honored guests at a dinner and a dance.

Source: Sonnichsen, 1974, p. 176.

14. For the complexities of Greene's personality see the chapter entitled "The Distorted Image" in Sonnichsen, 1974, pp. 258–69.

15. In 1897 Enrique Creel and Alfred A. Splendore organized the Ferrocarril de Chihuahua al Pacífico to build a line from Chihuahua City to the Pacific Ocean. They began building in March 1898 and reached Miñaca on May 20, 1900. That same year Arthur E. Stilwell was granted a concession to build, through his Ferrocarril Kansas City, Mexico and Orient, a line from Ojinaga to Chihuahua to Topolobampo. In 1902 Stilwell purchased the Chihuahua al Pacífico; thus the Stilwell railroad to which Parker alludes. Creel became connected

with the Stilwell interests at that time. This was the line that Parker had to use while he was operating at La República. In 1906 this railroad was extended northward to Temósachic.

In 1907 Greene, having acquired control of the Río Grande, Sierra Madre and Pacific in 1904, extended the line from Juárez to Casas Grandes and Terrazas, and he received concessions to build southward from Terrazas to Madera and from Madera to Temósachic. Parker was correct in stating that a connection was made between Terrazas and Madera, but it did not come until 1910, after Greene had given up control of the railroad.

Source: Almada, 1958, pp. 206–7; Sonnichsen, 1974, pp. 157, 221, 223; McNeely, 1965, pp. 20–21.

16. Perhaps Parker is in error here. The only Chávez that is revealed in the literature of the early revolution is Joaquin Chávez who lived at San Isidro. Chávez was a bullion contractor, as were Orozco and Villa, and one of his contracts was with Enrique Creel. Moreover, he was the commander of the Chihuahua City public security police force and as such was the recipient of many favors from the Creel-Terrazas-Díaz powers. Chávez, then, was a privileged business competitor to Orozco and Villa. At least one source credits the personal animosity between Chávez and Orozco as the reason the latter joined Madero against Díaz.

Orozco announced his revolution on November 19, 1910, at San Isidro. The following day he assaulted Miñaca with a force of forty-one men and captured the town. His next move was to return to San Isidro to attack the house of Joaquin Chávez who was defended by a personal guard of forty Tarahumara Indians. The Tarahumaras and Chávez were easy prey for Orozco's fanatics. The accounts do not specifically record the fact, but the implication is that Joaquin Chávez died at this time in his house.

This might not be the same Chávez that Parker is recording memories about, but no other Chávez who is a "bullion conductor" shows up in the literature of the early phases of the revolution. Parker's recollection of the three muleteers, Chávez, Orozco, and Villa, working together is romantic, but it does not accurately reflect what happened later. Orozco killed Chávez early and worked only a short time with Villa before starting his own revolution against Madero. Villa stayed with Madero and helped drive Orozco from Mexico.

Source: Santos, 1955, p. 65; Meyer, 1967, pp. 17, 19, 61.

THE REVOLUTION:
TRAILS, MULETEERS AND GENERALISIMOS

1. For detailed summaries of these events see Almada, 1964; Ross, 1955; and de Wetter, 1946. Personal though somewhat romanticized accounts of the battle of Juárez are found in Garibaldi, 1935, pp. 221–50, and Bush 1939, 201–11. For another El Pasoan's observations, see Sweeney, 1972, pp. 68–73.

2. Abraham González was forty-five years of age when the Maderistas successfully beseiged Juárez. He was described as a "portly, paternal man who had an unmistakable air of kindly authority. There was a twinkle of humor in his eyes, but this only served to emphasize the fires of faith burning behind them, which an occasional metallic glint amply confirmed. His followers were devoted to him, and he was unquestionably one of the best men Madero had around him. Would that there had been more of his type!" Thus wrote Garibaldi, 1935, p. 222. For the full history see Beezley, 1973.

3. Juan J. Navarro was born at Alamos, Sonora, in 1841. Joining the Sonora National Guard in 1859, he rose successively until he became Chief of the Army in 1913, two years after the encounter at Juárez. Navarro died in Mexico City on October 25, 1934.

   Source: Almada, 1968, p. 359.

4. A contemporary account was that Tamborrel had issued a statement to the effect that Madero's men were "a bunch of cowards." After the battle he was found lying on a bed with his hands tied behind him and a bullet hole through his head. At the head of his bed a large picture of Porfirio Díaz had been carefully placed. Judge Joseph Sweeney states that he was "shot in one leg, through his sword hand, through the breast, and through the head almost immediately between the eyes."

  Source: de Wetter, 1946, pp. 58–59; Sweeney, 1972, p. 71.

5. Garibaldi tells his own story in *A Toast to Rebellion* (Indianapolis: Bobbs-Merrill, 1935). Nicknamed "Peppino," he was born in Melbourne, Australia, fought in six wars, and was jailed by the Fascists before he escaped to the United States in 1924. He remained in voluntary exile until 1940, and he died in Rome on May 19, 1950.

  Source: New York *Times*, May 20, 1950, p. 15, c.3.

6. Interestingly, Garibaldi does not give Benjamin Johannis Viljoen a good report. In what could be a feeling of jealousy, the Italian writes:

> Among the new arrivals who attached themselves gratuitously to Madero was a General Viljoen, a Boer from the Transvaal and a veteran of the South African War. He arrived immediately after the Battle of Juarez and happened to be present in the room when Orozco threatened Madero. Naturally enough he was one of those to interfere, and afterward he declared that he was military adviser to the President. In this imaginary capacity he gave out a number of interviews, but we regarded him as a harmless crank. We were wrong, however. Through another Boer named De Villiers he arranged to have a telegram sent to him requesting an immediate interview on a matter of the greatest importance. To impress Madero he told him confidentially that the result of this talk was an offer of fifty thousand dollars if he would betray the President into federal hands. Viljoen offered to

set a trap for De Villiers and his associate, W. T. Dunn. This was done, and the police in El Paso arrested the two men. However, the American border police soon saw through the yarn and released the prisoners. Needless to say we had no further trouble from Viljoen.

The fact of the matter was that De Villiers was arrested on charges of conspiracy, indicted by a grand jury at El Paso, and released on bond.

Once the war with the British was ended, Viljoen was in the United States in time to exhibit his horsemanship in the Louisiana Purchase Exposition at St. Louis in 1904. Then he settled for a year at San Pablo de Machki, Chihuahua, before moving to Chamberino, near Las Cruces, New Mexico. There, with his two brothers, Chris and Weine, he farmed irrigated lands and was active in the Masonic Lodge and the Republican Party. After his service with Madero, Viljoen was appointed Commissioner to the Yaqui Indians. He went to Sonora to settle differences but did not remain long. He died at La Mesa, New Mexico, in 1917 and was buried in Las Cruces in the Masonic Cemetery.

Source: Garibaldi, 1935, p. 303; Olk, The Boers (undated typescript); El Paso *Times*, May 29, 1911, and May 30, 1911, and June 8, 1911.

7. Oscar Creighton was known as "The Dynamite Devil" as he captured the fancy of Madero and his army with daring deeds. Creighton had joined the Maderistas early and had fought northward almost to Juárez. While the army was camped south of Casas Grandes, Creighton was sent up the railroad tracks toward Corralitos to blow up the tracks to prevent the arrival of additional Federales. Creighton battled admirably until his death in the Battle of Bauche, a small railroad station just south of Ciudad Juárez. At a time when the Federales and Maderistas were stalemated in battle, Creighton, seeing a part of the Maderista line waver along the crest of a little hill, rushed up to steady his men, refusing to conceal himself.

Garibaldi described the scene:

> Standing fully erect with his poncho blowing in the wind, he was pumping lead from his Winchester at the advancing federals, when a bullet pierced his heart. The men, seeing him fall, were so enraged that they sprang forward and charged the oncoming enemy. With this action the federal rout began, and we pursued them almost to the town of Juarez. Even in death the brave American Captain had accomplished his purpose.
>
> It was dark when we finished leaving the battlefield and I had Captain Creighton buried beside the railroad track, so that we could locate the grave and give him a more fitting burial later on. The fifteenth of April, 1911, the date of the battle of Bauche . . . shall forever be symbolized in my mind by the heroic figure of Captain Creighton.

Garibaldi thought Creighton's appearance was "anything but prepossessing, though he was tall and well proportioned." His face was "extraordinarily homely" in that his head was crowned with "a thick mop of unkempt red hair" and his "receding chin was covered by a tangled red beard." In between he displayed blue-gray eyes that were "set too far apart" and "no nose worth the name: merely a small knob" above the upper lip. But this Creighton was a fighting man when alive and from such stuff legends are created. Ernest Schuster wrote that he had robbed several banks in the San Francisco area and had joined the revolution in Mexico to prove to his fiancee "what sort of man he really was." His body was brought across the international bridge with much pomp and ceremony in military fashion so it could be sent home to Boston. Thus Creighton ranged from Boston to San Francisco and points south, but his most lasting effect was perhaps on Pancho Villa who idolized Creighton — and learned from "The Dynamite Devil" some explosive techniques he later applied with felicity.

Source: Garibaldi, 1935, pp. 240, 277, 298–99; Schuster, 1947, unpaged introduction.

8. The story Parker tells about Kosterlitzky is significant for the folkloric tradition it perpetuates. In fact, Kosterlitzky had enlisted in the Mexican army at Guaymas on May 1, 1873, and had served Díaz's government until Don Porfirio left Mexico for France. In June 1911, he attempted to resign, but Madero wanted him to remain in the army as commander of the Third Military Zone of Sonora. He retired on February 12, 1912, but was still (or back?) on duty by May 1, when he participated in a skirmish with Orozquistas at La Dura. Finally, on March 13, 1913, Kosterlitzky left Mexico at Nogales, never to return. He died at Los Angeles, California, on March 2, 1928.

   Though Kosterlitzky served Madero's government, there is no evidence to show that he had any sympathy for the revolution, as he had been a loyal follower of Porfirio Díaz for too long. Nor is there evidence to show that he came to Juárez in 1911. And the story that he defected owing to a frightened mule is entirely legendary.

   Source: Smith, 1970, pp. 31, 37, 173, 176.

9. See Licéaga, 1958.

10. Villa's attack on Columbus, New Mexico, took place on March 9, 1916. See Braddy, 1965, and Harris and Sadler, 1975, pp. 335–46.

11. The other half of Parker and Parker was James H., older brother of Morris. James H. Parker was born in 1868 at Parker's Landing near Pen Yan, New York, the first child of Erastus Wells and Emmeline Brown Parker. He attended Colorado College at Colorado Springs, Colorado, and became a mining engineer. For a time he traveled and eventually married Olive Shelden of Manhattan, Kansas, around 1903. The couple had two children, both daughters, named Barbara and Virginia. They settled in El Paso in 1908 where James joined his brother, Morris, in a partnership, Parker and Parker, Mining Engineer Consultants, which they maintained for some twenty years. In 1915 he was a director of the El Paso Tin Mining and Smelting Company.

Parker, according to an obituary, had two loves — minerals and mining. He always had a small, choice collection of minerals. Arthur Montgomery wrote:

> He was full of warm friendliness, yet behind it lay impeccable dignity and old-world courtesy seldom found anymore. Behind that again, underneath the spectacles if you really cared to look for it, there was apt to be a twinkle of shy humor. Careful in his dress, as neat away from the haunts of men as among them, he was a gentleman of the old school if there ever was one.

James Parker died on April 29, 1948, while visiting in Houston, Texas. He was buried on May 3 in Evergreen Cemetery in El Paso, with services being conducted by the Reverend Stewart Hartfelter of El Paso's First Presbyterian Church. Olive Shelden Parker died May 5, 1969. The extensive files Parker compiled on mines and mining activities now form the bulk of the Southwestern Mining File of the El Paso Public Library.

Source: Montgomery, 1948, pp. 616–17; *Arizona Mining Journal*, December 26, 1928, p. 33; *Mexican Mining Journal*, January 1910, p. 40, and October 1910, p. 39; El Paso *Times*, May 1, 1948, and May 3, 1948; El Paso County Clerk, Probate File #20,710.

12. For variations on the way González died see Beezley, 1973, p. 159.

13. Born in Chihuahua City on August 30, 1854, Enrique Creel has been a much praised and much maligned man. Praise has come to him because of his strength in politics, business, and cultural activities. Creel wrote *El Estado de Chihuahua: Su Historia, Geografía, y Riquezas Naturales* (Mexico: Tip. el progreso, 1928), and was the organizer of the Tenth International Geological Congress in 1906, founder of the Astronomical Society of Mexico, president of the Mexican Geographic

and Statistical Society. He was responsible for the establish-ment of the Chihuahua State Mining Exposition in 1906 and for the appointment of George Griggs as director of it. When presidents William Howard Taft of the United States and Porfirio Díaz of Mexico met in El Paso in October 1909, Creel acted as interpreter. For his cultural activities, Creel received an honorary doctor of law degree from the University of Pennsylvania.

He was likewise a giant in business as president of the Company of Telephones of Chihuahua and Durango, presi-dent of the Banco Central de Mexico, president of the Com-pañía del Ferrocarril Mineral de Santa Eulalia, councillor for the Batopilas Mining Company, founder and president of the Banco Agrícola Hipotecario de México, vice-president of the Kansas City, Mexico and Orient Railroad, and other titles almost into infinity. Creel was the first president of the Chamber of Commerce of Chihuahua and saw in his state the opportunity to consolidate it as an industrial power.

As a politician Creel was the symbol of Porfirio Díaz in the state, all the good and all the bad. Creel was governor of Chihuahua from 1903 through 1910, up to the eve of the Madero revolution. Creel married a daughter of Don Luis Terrazas, Sr., and along with the marriage came the oppor-tunity for politics and wealth. Creel made the best of his opportunities as he became the seventeenth governor of his state.

Creel's father was Ruben W. Creel, American consul in Chihuahua and a descendant of a Kentucky aristocratic family, and his mother was Doña Paz Cuilty, of good Chihuahua family, but of Spanish blood mixed with Indian. When the revolutionaries of Madero approached the subject of Enrique Creel, they did so with the same hatred they reserved for Porfirio Díaz and Luis Terrazas, Sr. Creel was of southern aristocratic and Indian blood, they were fond of saying, a half breed by birth and wholly Mexican by inclination. Like many "breeds," he "inherited the vices of both races and the virtues of neither." After the Madero revolutionaries were successful, the Creel and Terrazas interests put some of their money behind Pascual Orozco and his counter-revolution which failed. But with the revolution Creel's most active days were ended. After the fighting, he returned to his native land, where he died in Mexico City on August 17, 1931. Much has been written about him, but the definitive biography awaits the scholar.

Source: Almada, 1968, p. 124; Almada, 1950, pp. 437–47; Sandels, 1967, pp. vii, 31–39; Griggs, 1911, between pp. 290–92; Bush, 1939, pp. 164–65.

14. See Braddy, 1966.

YAQUI INDIANS AND MY ESCAPE
FROM REVOLUTIONARIES

1. Parker is writing here about the Sonora and Sinaloa Irrigation Company which was chartered in New York in 1891 to dam and exploit the waters of the Yaqui River. Carlos Conant was the prime mover of the organization which had as officers Walter S. Logan, president; W. A. Watson, vice-president; S. S. Clark, secretary. E. S. Nettleton of Denver, Colorado, was consulting engineer, and T. H. Todd was engineer in charge.
   Source: Dabdoud, 1964, pp. 277–93; Hu-Dehart, pp. 76–77.

2. This particular aspect of the Yaqui war began in 1897 and continued until 1914 when the remaining Yaquis joined forces with Pancho Villa. The picture Parker provides is graphic enough, but not unusual. An intensive drive to round-up the Yaquis began in 1901, and by 1904, according to United States Ambassador Powell Clayton, "the great bulk of the Yaqui

Indians had been deported from Sonora to Yucatan." But the trouble continued as testified to by none other than Emilio Kosterlitzky in 1906:

> I want to say something about the "Yaqui trouble" of which we have heard so much lately. There is no war with the Yaquis in Mexico. I wish there were and that the Indians would show themselves. But they are like deer, scattering when approached. General Torres took the field recently, but found that chasing Yaquis was like chasing a will-o-the-wisp.

In spite of the deportations and killings, small bands of Yaquis were still fighting as late as 1927. At that time the government relented and the Yaquis began to return home to follow their old way of life. They were made legitimate in 1939 when the Mexican government set aside for them twenty percent of their old land.

Source: Almada, 1952, pp. 335–36; United States Congress, *Papers Relating . . .*, 1969, pp. 639–49; Giddings, 1959, pp. 7–8; Smith, 1970, pp. 120–21; Acuña, 1974, p. 139.

3. The Fortuna-North Tigre claims included the mines named Santa María, Ventura, Fortuna, and North Tigre. Parker apparently became consulting engineer in 1909 but he inspected the property in December 1908, as the following article in that month's *El Paso Mining Journal* (p. 7) indicates:

> Morris B. Parker, the well known El Paso mining engineer, has returned from a business trip to Imuris, Son., where he examined the Santa Gertrudes and the Espirito properties. These mines are south of the Sierra Azul, and the trip is made via Guaymas. Mr. Parker brought back considerable ore from these properties, and among other things he is showing some magnificent specimens of rhodochrosite and pyrolousite. Mr. Parker states that business is improving steadily and that on his trip he noted at the hotels and on the trains numbers of mining men and investors, denoting that the metal mining industry is especially going

ahead. He also states that every mining man of the western portion of Old Mexico is taking a long breath of relief because of the probability of the ending of the Yaqui troubles. Mr. Parker is now at La Fortuna mine in the El Tigre section.

Parker made an extensive report to the stockholders in April 1910, one which drew graphic word pictures of the shafts, stopes and winzes and concluded with the hope that sales of treasury stock in the immediate future would permit the building of a mill. The present stockholders were asked to "urge their friends and acquaintances to invest in this stock." By March 1911, the Fortuna ore shipped to the ASARCO smelter at El Paso amounted to 1998 tons and brought a profit of $22.57 per ton. To get this the company had done about 1600 feet of development work.

Source: Parker, 1910; *Mexican Mining Journal*, March 1911, p. 42.

4. This mine was known as the Lucky Tiger and its shafts crossed the property lines of the Fortuna company. The Lucky Tiger opened in 1903 and through 1909 had grossed $3,442,683.73. Net profit for the year 1909 was $586,597.99 with actual ore reserves of 256,891 tons. Plans at that time called for increasing the mill capacity to 250 tons per day with the addition of a 250 ton Cyanide Plant. During 1910 the mine produced a net value of $915,036.06 at a cost of $343,710.21. The mine was still producing in 1915 at which time it was the third largest in Sonora, trailing only Cananea and Nacozari.

Source: Parker, 1910; *Mexican Mining Journal*, June 1911, p. 34; Bernstein, 1965, pp. 70–71; Parker, 1908, pp. 19–20.

5. Possibly Cenobio Rivera Domínguez. See Rivera, 1969, p. 398.

6. This campaign is adequately covered in Rivera, 1969, pp. 419–52.

7. Parker has described the confiscation of this mine in the chapter entitled "Hacienda Durazo, Sonora." By September 1910, the Cinco de Mayo was being expanded by Herman, King and Associates under a contract with Francisco H. García, its owner. As workers were expanding on the seventh level in November, they struck a bonanza of chlorides and native silver. By February 1911, the company was extracting two to five tons of high grade ore daily which averaged from 250 to 400 ounces of silver per ton. In 1913 the mine was seized by revolutionaries, who operated it. In July of that year they sent a carload of ore to the smelter at Douglas and sold it for $8,000. Whether Calles was able to operate it or not cannot be discerned, but Joe Adair tried to make it function profitably in 1916 and gave it up owing to banditry.

   Source: *Mexican Mining Journal*, September 1910, pp. 34, 37; November 1910, p. 38; February 1911, p. 37; March 1911, p. 31; August 1913, p. 403; and April 1916, p. 135.

8. George Wiley Paul Hunt (1859–1934) was a native of Missouri. He came to Arizona in 1881, settling as a rancher on the Salt River. In 1891 he went to work for the Dominican Commercial Company in Globe and by 1900 was president of the company. He was the first mayor of Globe after its incorporation, served in the Arizona Territorial House of Representatives in 1893 and 1895, served in the Territorial Senate, 1897–1901 and 1905–1911. From 1905 to 1909 Hunt served as presiding officer of the Senate. In 1910 he was president of Arizona's Constitutional Convention, afterward being elected the first governor of the state. From 1912 to 1932 he ran for governor nine times, losing only in 1918 and 1928. He retired from office in 1932. Hunt was in his second term as governor when Parker called on him for assistance.

   Source: Goff, 1973; Brown, 1962, p. 3; Sparks, Bateman and Brandes, 1961, p. 17; Kartus, 1931, pp. 39–43.

9. William C. McDonald had tutored Parker in geometry at White Oaks when Parker was a youngster. Moreover, McDonald was the stepfather of Parker's wife. In sending to McDonald for help Parker was on safe grounds. McDonald died in El Paso on April 10, 1918 and was buried at the White Oaks cemetery.

    Source: Sonnichsen, 1971, pp. xvii, 44, 58; El Paso *Herald*, April 11, 1918.

10. This hotel was built in 1906 by the Douglas Investment Company. Often referred to as one of the finest hotels in the state, it burned in October 1928, and was replaced by one designed by Trost and Trost, architects of El Paso.

    Source: Bond, 1975, p. 29.

AFTER THE REVOLUTION:
LOS TEJONES, NAYARIT, AND CANANEA, SONORA

1. Isoroku Yamamoto, born in April 1884, was a well educated individual who at age thirty was adopted by the wealthy Yamamoto family. In 1917–1918 he came to America to study at Harvard University. His subject was the oil industry of the United States, but he was also interested in mining and he made a journey through Mexico. Perhaps it was this experience that caused him to become connected with the company that attempted to develop Los Tejones.

    From 1925 to 1927 Yamamoto was naval attaché in the Japanese embassy in Washington and he represented Japan at naval conferences in London in 1930 and 1933. He planned the Japanese attack on Pearl Harbor, December 7, 1941, only to be killed by American fighter pilots on April 18, 1943.

    Source: Potter, 1965, pp. 4, 14–22, 301–7.

2. San Blas was established as a Spanish seaport in 1768 by order of José de Galvéz. Father Junípero Serra used it as a base of supply for his missions in Baja California and later in California. Because of this the town became famous for its bells which rang from the towers of missions throughout the Southwest. Henry Wadsworth Longfellow romanticized the bells in a poem, but the bells do not tell the whole story. Under the Spaniards, San Blas was the principal port on the northwest coast of Mexico, the control of which was considered essential in the War of Independence, 1810–1811. Its importance as a seaport continued through the nineteenth century, but it was just a quiet town of fishermen when Parker was there.

   Source: Gulick, 1965, pp. 88–90.

3. The story of Cananea is easily and excellently available in Sonnichsen, 1974.

4. The standard, though adulatory, work is Millon, 1966.

5. Chalcocite is the richest combination of copper with sulphur. In its hard, steely form it is called "copper glance."

   Source: Joralemon, 1935, p. 279.

6. More recently spelled San Javier. At the heart of this district is the pueblo of San Javier, which had a population of about four hundred persons when Parker was there. Founded in 1706 by General Antonio Becera Nieto, it is located at the junction of the Arroyo de Las Lajas and the Tecoripa River. In addition to the mines Parker mentions, nearby were the La Barranca, Goteras, and El Tarahumara. Also the Ohio-Yaqui Mining Company managed by James S. Lawrence developed the Sierra Mine.

   Source: Almada, 1952, pp. 718–19; *Mexican Mining Journal*, September 1909, p. 30, and October 1909, p. 39.

7. An unnamed correspondent in 1911 noted that the outlook at San Javier was "brightening" owing to activity at the Buena Vista, Las Animas, and Las Goteras. Four years later another unnamed writer noted the "extensive mining regions with historic records" which included the camps at San Javier, La Barranca, Los Bronces, San Antonio de la Huerta, Las Goteras, Cerro Colorado, San Juan Grande, and Soyopa. He continued: "At San Javier the Gold Coin Mining Co. has a 30-ton copper smelter. This company also owns the Santa Rosa, a well-known antigua. At the same place the Wyman Mining Co., operating the Animas mine, has erected a 50-ton concentrating plant. The Verde Grande is a copper property near San Javier."

   Source: *Mexican Mining Journal*, April 1911, p. 35, and July 1915, p. 249.

8. Dahlgren, 1883, p. 71, spells the name "Alsua" and notes the fact that his headquarters are at Los Bronces, where Alzua had a twenty-stamp mill.

9. The Los Bronces mine was owned by Mexico's Vice-President, Ramón Corral, in 1910 and was operated under lease by J. F. and C. R. Williams. It mined coal, which was in demand by mine operators for fuel and commanded a high price, from a vein fourteen feet wide. The company had thirty-five men on the payroll. Also at Los Bronces the Carmen Mining Company was operating the Carmen Mine.

   Source: *Mexican Mining Journal*, September 1909, p. 30, and September 1910, p. 38, and October 1910, p. 38.

10. As early as 1909 the Wyman Mining Company was operating the Animas Mine with Frank Davis as manager and Edward George as superintendent. At that time they had $1,000,000 worth of ore blocked out and were erecting a concentrating plant. By the next year they had 2,000,000 ounces of silver blocked out in ore running from forty to four hundred ounces to the ton. A 1913 account gives a picture of the extensiveness of the operation:

Las Animas. — The property during the past two years has produced $200,000 in ore and concentrates, under the management of W. C. Laughlin. The output has been shipped to the El Paso smelter. In addition to this the company has mined $400,000 worth of ore which is on the dumps. The company is at present using 1,000 pack animals conveying ore and concentrates from the San Xavier properties to Toledo, the shipping point on the Tonichi branch of the Southern Pacific Railroad. At the present time there is more activity in the camp than has been experienced for a number of years. The Yaqui indians seemingly not interfering with the operation of the mines. The company is shipping from five to seven carloads of ore weekly to the El Paso smelter.

Source: *Mexican Mining Journal*, September 1909, p. 33; September 1910, p. 37; December 1912, pp. 45, 48; February 1913, p. 97; and April 1913, p. 203.

11. In 1909 the Santa Rosa was operated by the Gold Coin Santa Rosa Mining Company. It had a smelting plant ready to operate "as soon as transportation facilities are improved."
    Source: *Mexican Mining Journal*, September 1909, p. 33.

12. The patio process was perfected in 1557 by Bartolomé Medina of Pachuca to solve the difficult problem of refining lead-silver sulphides. Heat and oxygen normally reduced sulphides of silver and copper to the pure metal and gaseous sulphur dioxide, but Medina found that the normal process would not work on the ore of Pachuca. The process he developed to solve the problem is described as follows:

> This process began by grinding the ore into middling sized sands, washing away the country rock, then spreading the residue thinly on a stone platform or patio. Large quantities of salt, copper sulphate (bluestone), and mercury were then added and worked in. Indian labor at first did the mixing and trampling, but quadrupeds were soon employed, since the crude ammonias so liberally contributed to the mix by horses and mules improved the quantity

of the yield. From time to time, the mix or *lama* was spread thinly, and uniformly about the patio for exposure to heat and sunlight, then it was heaped into a mound or *torta* and let stand before another redistribution. The mix changed gradually to a grey color, and fifteen to forty-five days later was judged finished. It was then washed, and the mercury-silver amalgam recovered and retorted.

Source: Young 1965, pp. 307–8.

13. The La Dura Mining Company took over this famous mine in 1880 and operated it until 1910 at which time it passed to the Mines Company of America. In 1909 the mine worked about five hundred men. Early in 1912 there were half a dozen American companies starting development work adjacent to the mine at a time when general conditions were good. The country was quiet and there was no dissatisfaction with governmental conditions and none was expected. Expected or not, the La Dura was forced to close in the fall of 1913 because of the hardship involved in securing supplies and other difficulties without number. But the ore in La Dura was too rich for it to remain idle for long and it was made functional after revolutionary activity ceased.

Source: "Mexican Mining in 1913," 1914, p. 137; Brinegar, 1910, p. 27; *Mexican Mining Journal*, May 1909, p. 31; October 1910, p. 38; February 1912, p. 49; December 1912, p. 48; and March 1914, p. 133.

14. George A. Schroeter and W. C. Laughlin are the two men involved. In January 1910, Schroeter was consulting engineer for the Lluvia de Oro Company in Chihuahua but by October held a similar position with the Mines Company of America at La Dura. In addition, he served as managing engineer for the Victoria Gold Mining Company which owned the Esmeralda Mine near Minas Prieta.

At the beginning of 1910 Laughlin was manager for the Barrancas Mines (Mexico) Ltd., of London, at their mines near San Javier which included the Las Goteras. The Schroe-ter-Laughlin lease was for the Las Animas Mine owned by Wyman Mining Company but leased from them in 1911 and managed by Laughlin, who had made a great success in the operations by 1913. In January of that year, Laughlin shipped $200,000 worth of ore and concentrates to the smelter at El Paso and he had another $400,000 ready to ship in February.

Source: *Mexican Mining Journal*, January 1910, pp. 10, 35; April 1911, p. 35; December 1912, p. 45; and February 1913, p. 97.

Bibliography

BOOKS

Ackerman, Carl W.
   1930   *George Eastman*. Boston: Houghton Mifflin Company.

Acuña, Rodolfo F.
   1974   *Sonoran Strongman: Ignacio Pesqueira and His Times*. Tucson: University of Arizona Press.

Almada, Francisco R.
   1927   *Diccionario de Historia, Geografía y Biografía Chihuahuenses*. Chihuahua: Talleres Gráficos del Gobierno del Estado.

   1950   *Gobernadores del Estado de Chihuahua*. Mexico, D. F.: Imprenta de la H. Camara Diputado.

   1952   *Diccionario de Historia, Geografía y Biografía Sonorenses*. Chihuahua: Arrentatarios De Impresora Ruiz Sandoval.

   1964   *La Revolución en el Estado de Chihuahua*. Mexico, D. F.: Talleres Gráficos en la Nación.

   1968   *Diccionario de Historia, Geografía y Biografía Chihuahuenses*. 2nd edition. Chihuahua: Universidad de Chihuahua Departamento de Investigaciones Sociales Sección de Historia.

Atlas Geográfico
   1966   *Atlas Geográfico de la República Mexicana*. Mexico, D. F.: Ediciones Ateneo.

Barrett, Ward
   1970   *The Sugar Hacienda of the Marqueses Del Valle*. Minneapolis: University of Minnesota Press.

Beezley, William H.
   1973   *Insurgent Governor: Abraham González and the Mexican Revolution in Chihuahua.* Lincoln: University of Nebraska Press.

Bennett, Wendell C. and Robert M. Zingg
   1935   *The Tarahumara: An Indian Tribe of Northern Mexico.* Chicago: University of Chicago Press.

Bernstein, Marvin D.
   1965   *The Mexican Mining Industry, 1890–1950.* Albany, New York: State University of New York.

Bond, Ervin
   1975   *Douglas, Arizona: Its First Seventy-Five Years.* Douglas: By the Author.

Braddy, Haldeen
   1965   *Pancho Villa at Columbus: The Raid of 1916.* El Paso: Texas Western Press. Southwestern Studies Monograph No. 9.

   1966   *Pershing's Mission in Mexico.* El Paso: Texas Western Press.

   1970   *Cock of the Walk: The Legend of Pancho Villa.* Reprint. Port Washington, New York: Kennikat Press.

Bradley, Glenn Danford
   1920   *The Story of the Santa Fe.* Boston: Richard G. Badge.

Bush, I. J.
   1939   *Gringo Doctor.* Caldwell, Idaho: Caxton Printers.

Callicot, Wilfred Hardy
   1931   *Liberalism in Mexico, 1857–1929.* Palo Alto, California: Stanford University Press.

Caloca, Jesús Ramírez
   1955   *Nociones de Geografía del Estado de Chihuahua.* Chihuahua: Litografía "El Cromo."

Carson, Oliver, and Ernest Sutherland Bates
   1936   *Hearst, Lord of San Simeon.* New York: The Viking Press.

Cassell, Jonathan F.
   1969   *Tarahumara Indians.* San Antonio: Naylor.

Chávez M., Armando B.
   1959   *Síntesis Gráfica de la Historia de Ciudad Juárez.* Tricentenario de su Fundación.

Cleland, Robert Glass
   1952   *A History of Phelps Dodge, 1834–1950.* New York: Alfred A. Knopf.

Coan, Charles F.
   1925   *A History of New Mexico.* 3 vols.; Chicago: The American Historical Society.

Comstock, John Henry
   1913   *The Spider Book, A Manual for the Study of the Spiders and Their Near Relatives.* Garden City, New York: Doubleday, Page & Company.

Coolidge, Mary Roberts
   1909   *Chinese Immigration.* New York: Henry Holt and Company.

Creel, Enrique
   1928   *El Estado de Chihuahua: Su Historia, Geografía, y Riquezas Naturales.* Mexico, D. F.: Tip. el progreso.

Cumberland, Charles Curtis
   1952   *Mexican Revolution: Genesis Under Madero.* Austin: University of Texas Press.

Dabdoud, Claudio
   1964   *Historia de el Valle del Yaqui.* Mexico, D. F.: Librería Manuel Porrúa, S.A.

Dahlgren, Charles B.
   1883   *Historic Mines of Mexico: A Review of the Mines of That Republic for the Past Three Centuries.* New York: For the author.

Dana, Edward Salisbury
   1920   *Descriptive Mineralogy.* 6th ed. New York: John Wiley and Sons.

Diccionario Porrúa
   1971   *Diccionario Porrúa de Historia, Biografía y Geografía de Mexico.* 3d ed. 2 vols. Mexico, D. F.: Editorial Porrúa.

Douglas, James
   1910   *Journals and Reminiscences of James Douglas, M. D.* New York: Privately Printed.

Dunbier, Roger
   1968   *The Sonoran Desert: Its Geography, Economy, and People.* Tucson: University of Arizona Press.

Estado de Chihuahua
undated   *Estado de Chihuahua*. Impresa en los Talleres Gráficos de la Secretaría de Agricultura y Fomento. Map.

Evans and Worley
1898   *Evans and Worley's Directory of the City of El Paso, 1896–1897*. Dallas: John F. Worley & Co.

Fay, Albert A.
1947   *A Glossary of the Mining and Mineral Industry*. Reprint. Washington: Government Printing Office.

Flippin, J. O.
1889   *Sketches From the Mountains of Mexico*. Cincinnati: Standard Publishing Company.

Fretz, J. Winfield
1945   *Mennonite Colonization in Mexico*. Akron, Pennsylvania: The Mennonite Central Committee. Publication No. 2.

García y Alva, Federico, director y ed.
1905–07   *"Mexico y sus Progresos," Album-Directorio del Estado de Sonora: Obra hecha con apoyo del Gobierno del Estado*. Hermosillo: Imprenta Oficial Dirigida por Antonio B. Monteverde.

Garibaldi, Giuseppe
1935   *A Toast to Rebellion*. Indianapolis: Bobbs-Merrill.

Gelatt, Roland
1955   *The Fabulous Phonograph, From Tin Foil to High Fidelity*. Philadelphia: J. B. Lippincott.

Giddings, Ruth Warner
1959   *Yaqui Myths and Legends*. Tucson: University of Arizona Press.

Godoy, José F.
1910   *Porfirio Díaz, President of Mexico: The Master Builder of a Great Commonwealth*. New York: G. P. Putnam's Sons.

Goff, John S.
1973   *George W. P. Hunt and His Arizona*. Pasadena, California: Socio-Technical Publications.

Granger, Byrd H., rev.
1960   *Will C. Barnes' Arizona Place Names*. Tucson: University of Arizona Press.

Griggs, George
    1907   *Mines of Chihuahua.* Chihuahua: A. Vicente Guerrero.
    1911   *Mines of Chihuahua.* 3d ed. Chihuahua: Imp. El Norte.

Gulick, Howard E.
    1965   *Nayarit, Mexico: A Traveler's Guidebook.* Glendale, California: Arthur H. Clark.

Hall, Beaumont
    1949   *The Present Day.* New York: The Museum of Modern Art.

Hamilton, Leonides
    1882   *The Border States of Mexico: Sonora, Sinaloa, Chihuahua and Durango.* 3d ed. Chicago: Leonides Hamilton.

Hanay, David
    1917   *Díaz.* London: Constable and Company.

Heitman, Francis B.
    1903   *Historical Register and Dictionary of the United States Army from its Organization September 29, 1789, to March 2, 1903.* 2 vols. Washington: Government Printing Office.

History of the Baldwin
    1907   *History of the Baldwin Locomotive Works, 1831 to 1907.* Philadelphia: The Edgell Company.

Hodge, Frederick Webb
    1912   *Handbook of American Indians North of Mexico.* 2 vols. Washington: Government Printing Office.

Holden, W. C., ed.
    1936   "The Life and Doings of the Yaqui Indians of the San Ygnacio Yaqui River as furnished to Ivan Williams," *Studies of the Yaqui Indians of Sonora, Mexico.* Lubbock: Texas Technological College. Bulletin XIV, No. 1, Scientific Series No. 2.

Hunt, Frazier
    1938   *One American and His Attempt at Education.* New York: Simon and Schuster.

Joralemon, Ira B.
    1935   *Romantic Copper, Its Lure and Lore.* New York: D. Appleton-Century Company.
    1973   *Copper: The Encompassing Story of Mankind's First Metal.* Berkeley: Howell-North Books.

Kelly, Ralph
 1946   *Matthias W. Baldwin (1795–1866) Locomotive Pioneer.*
    New York: The Newcomer Society of England, Ameri-
    can Branch.

Kirkham, Stanton Davis
 1909   *Mexican Trails: A Record of Travel in Mexico, 1904–
    07, and a Glimpse at the Life of the Mexican Indian.*
    New York: G. P. Putnam's Sons.

Langton, H. H.
 1940   *James Douglas, A Memoir.* Toronto: University of
    Toronto Press.

Leland, Everard
 1930   *Mining Methods and Costs at the Pilares Mines, Pilares
    de Nacozari, Sonora, Mexico.* United States Bureau of
    Mines Information Circular 6307. Washington: Gov-
    ernment Printing Office.

Leonard, John William, ed.
 1922   *Who's Who in Engineering: A Biographical Dictionary
    of Contemporaries, 1922–1923.* New York: John W.
    Leonard Corp.

 1925   *Who's Who In Engineering: A Biographical Directory
    of Contemporaries, 1925.* Second edition. New York:
    Who's Who Publications, Inc.

Licéaga, Luis
 1958   *Félix Díaz.* Mexico, D. F.: Editorial Jus.

Lister, Florence C. and Robert H.
 1966   *Chihuahua: Storehouse of Storms.* Albuquerque: Uni-
    versity of New Mexico Press.

Logans, Jesús J., ed.
 1959   *Chihuahua: Ciudad Prócer.* Chihuahua: Universidad
    de Chihuahua y Sociedad Chihuahuenses de Estudios
    Históricos.

Lumholtz, Carl
 1903   *Unknown Mexico: A Record of Five Year's Explora-
    tion Among the Tribes of the Western Sierra Madre;
    in the Tierra Caliente of Tepic and Jalisco; and
    Among The Tarascos of Michoacán.* 2 vols. London:
    Macmillan and Company.

Lundberg, Ferdinand
    1937   *Imperial Hearst*: *A Social Biography*. New York: Random House Modern Library.

McBride, George McCutchen
    1971   *The Land Systems of Mexico*. Reprint. New York: Octagon Books.

Manual Informativo
    1909   *Manual Informativo del Estado de Chihuahua* (*Geografía, Recursos Naturales, Organización Política y Desarrollo Económico*).

Map of Moctezuma District
    1900   *Map of Moctezuma District, Sonora, July 22, 1900* (Mining File, Mexico, State of Sonora, District of Moctezuma, Folder 606–55, Southwest Reference, El Paso Public Library).

Marcosson, Isaac F.
    1949   *Metal Magic*: *The Story of the American Smelting & Refining Company*. New York: Farrar, Strauss and Company.

Marquis Who's Who
    1974   *Who's Who in America, 1974–1975*. 38th ed. Chicago: Marquis Who's Who.

Martin, Percy F.
    1907   *Mexico of the Twentieth Century*. 2 vols. London: Edward Arnold.

Mexican Yearbook, The
    1908   *The Mexican Yearbook 1908. Comprising Historical & Fiscal Information. Compiled From Official and Other Records*. London: McConquodale & Co.

Meyer, Michael C.
    1967   *Mexican Rebel*: *Pascual Orozco and the Mexican Revolution, 1910–1915*. Lincoln: University of Nebraska Press.

Millares, Jorge Hernández, and Alejandro Carmillo Escribano
    1966   *Atlas Porrúa de la República Mexicana*. Mexico: Editorial Porrúa, S. A.

Millon, Robert Paul
    1966   *Mexican Marxist*: *Vicente Lombardo Toledano*. Chapel Hill: University of North Carolina Press.

Myrick, David F.
    1970   *New Mexico's Railroads — An Historical Survey.*
            Golden, Colorado: Colorado Railroad Museum.

National Cyclopaedia, The
    1892–   *The National Cyclopaedia of American Biography.*
    1969   51 vols. New York: James T. White and Company.

Parker, Morris B.
    1910   *Consulting Engineer's Report on the Fortuna Mining
            Company's Properties to April, 1910.* In Mining File,
            Folder 606–38, Southwest Reference, El Paso Public
            Library.

Pfefferkorn, Ignaz (Theodore E. Trautlein, ed.)
    1949   *Sonora: A Description of the Province.* Albuquerque:
            University of New Mexico Press.

Pinchon, Edgcumb
    1933   *Viva Villa: A Recovery of the Real Pancho Villa.* New
            York: Grosset and Dunlap.

Pletcher, David M.
    1958   *Rails, Mines, and Progress: Seven American Promoters
            in Mexico, 1867–1911.* Ithaca, New York: Cornell Uni-
            versity Press.

Porter, Eugene O.
    1970   *Lord Beresford and Lady Flo.* El Paso: Texas Western
            Press. Southwestern Studies Monograph No. 25.

Potter, John Deane
    1965   *Yamamoto: The Man Who Menaced America.* New
            York: Viking Press.

Rivera, Antonio G.
    1969   *La Revolución en Sonora.* Mexico, D. F.: Imprenta
            Arana.

Roca, Paul M.
    1967   *Paths of the Padres Through Sonora, An Illustrated
            History and Guide to Its Spanish Cultures.* Tucson:
            Arizona Pioneer's Historical Society.

Romero, Matías
    1898   *Geographical and Statistical Notes on Mexico.* New
            York: G. P. Putnam's Sons.

Romney, Thomas Gotham
    1938   *The Mormon Colonies in Mexico.* Salt Lake City: The
            Deseret Book Store.

Ross, Stanley R.
1955 *Francisco I. Madero, Apostle of Mexican Democracy.*
New York: Columbia University Press.

Rouaix, Ing. Pastor
1946 *Diccionario Geográfico, Histórico y Biográfico del
Estado de Durango.* Mexico: Panamericano de Geografía e Historia.

Rowse, Edward
1976 *Concord's Wagon Men.* Privately Printed.

Santos, Daniel Gutiérrez
1955 *Historia Militar de México, 1876–1914.* Mexico: Ediciones Citoneo.

Schuster, Ernest Otto
1947 *Pancho Villa's Shadow.* New York: The Exposition
Press.

Seton, Ernest Thompson
1953 *Lives of Game Animals.* Reprint. 4 vols. Boston:
Charles T. Branford Company.

Shepherd, Grant
1938 *The Silver Magnet: Fifty Years in a Mexican Silver
Mine.* New York: E. P. Dutton & Co.

Smith, Cornelius C., Jr.
1970 *Emilio Kosterlitzky: Eagle of Sonora and the Southwest
Border.* Glendale, California: Arthur H. Clark.

Sonnichsen, C. L.
1971 *Morris B. Parker's White Oaks: Life in a New Mexico
Gold Camp, 1880–1900.* Tucson: University of Arizona
Press.

1974 *Colonel Greene and the Copper Skyrocket.* Tucson:
University of Arizona Press.

Swanberg, W. A.
1961 *Citizen Hearst: A Biography of William Randolph
Hearst.* New York: Charles Scribner's Sons.

Terry, T. Philip
1947 *Terry's Guide to Mexico.* Rev. ed. Boston: Rapid Service Press.

Treutlein, Theodore E., trans.
1965 *Missionary in Sonora: The Travel Reports of Joseph
Och, S. J., 1755–1767.* San Francisco: California Historical Society.

Twitchell, Ralph Emerson
    1917   *The Leading Facts of New Mexican History.* 5 vols. Cedar Rapids, Iowa: The Torch Press.

United States Congress
    1933   *Congressional Record, First Session, Seventy-Third Congress of the United States, May 26, 1933 to June 7, 1933.* Washington: Government Printing Office.

    1969   *Papers Relating to the Foreign Relations of the United States with the Annual Message of the President Transmitted to the Congress December 5, 1905.* Reprint. New York: Kraus Reprint Company. No. 4941 in serial set.

Watts, Peter
    1977   *A Dictionary of the Old West, 1850–1900.* New York: Alfred A. Knopf.

Whetten, Nathan L.
    1948   *Rural Mexico.* Chicago: University of Chicago Press.

Winter, Nevin O.
    1907   *Mexico and Her People of To-Day.* Boston: L. C. Page & Co.

PERIODICALS

Anderson, Charles McC.
    1908   "On the Trail Through Western Chihuahua," *Mexican Mining Journal* (November): 11–14.

Beverly, Walter D.
    1909   "Reminiscences of Mining in Durango," *Engineering and Mining Journal* (October 2): 635–39.

Boyd, Alfred O. as told to Eve Ball
    1963   "Lady Flo," *Frontier Times* (February-March): 34–35, 44.

Brown, Leonard E.
    1962   "Arizona's State Governors," *Arizoniana* (Spring): 3–9.

Coll, A.
    1911   "Opening the Moctezuma District," *Mining and Scientific Press* (January 11): 14.

El Paso Electric Company
    1921   *Cactus Points* (September), unpaged.

"Geronimo's Maddest Outrage"
    1908   "Geronimo's Maddest Outrage," *El Paso Mining Journal* (October): unpaged.

Graham, T. C.
    1911   "Northern District of Durango," *Mexican Mining Journal* (June): 33–34.

Harris, Charles H., III, and Louis R. Sadler
    1975   "Pancho Villa and the Columbus Raid: The Missing Documents," *New Mexico Historical Review* (October): 335–46.

Hu-Dehart, Evelyn
    1974   "Development and Rural Rebellion: Pacification of the Yaquis in the Late Porfiriato," *Hispanic American Historical Review* (February): 72–93.

Hutchinson, Spencer W.
    1906   "Mining in Western Chihuahua," *Engineering and Mining Journal* (March 3): 418–20.

"James Stuart Douglas"
    1918   "James Stuart Douglas," *Engineering and Mining Journal* (July 6): 18–20.

Kartus, Sidney
    1931   "Helen Duett Ellison Hunt (Mrs. George W. P. Hunt)," *The Arizona Historical Review* (July): 39–43.

Katz, Friedrick
    1974   "Labor Conditions on Haciendas in *Porfirian* Mexico: Some Trends and Tendencies," *Hispanic American Historical Review* (February): 1–47.

Kline, R. G.
    1911   "Treatment of Silver Ores at Guanaceví, Mexico," *Mining and Scientific Press* (March 18): 402–5.

Lamb, Mark R.
    1908   "Hacienda Buburon, An Old Silver Mill," *Engineering and Mining Journal* (October 3): 663–64.

Layton, H. B.
    1900   "The Nacosari Mines, Mexico," *Engineering and Mining Journal* (June 9): 678–79.

    1900   "The Nacosari Mines, Mexico," *Engineering and Mining Journal* (June 16): 707.

Linton, Robert
    1912   "Historical Sketch of the Ocampo Mines," *Engineering and Mining Journal* (September 7): 457–59.

"A Man Who Died . . ."
    1909   "A Man Who Died to Save a Town," *Harper's Weekly* (March 20): 29.

Merrill, J. H.
    1910   "Sonora, Mexico, in 1909," *Mining and Scientific Press* (January 22): 157.

"Mexican Mining in 1913"
    1914   "Mexican Mining in 1913," *Engineering and Mining Journal* (January 10): 137.

Montgomery, Arthur
    1948   "Mr. [James] Parker," *Rocks and Minerals* (July): 616–17.

Nelson, C. N.
    1903   "A Trip Through Northern Durango," *Engineering and Mining Journal* (April 3): 697–98.

Pace, Anne
    1974   "Mexican Refugees in Arizona, 1910–1911," *Arizona and the West* (Spring): 5–18.

Parker, M. B.
    1908   "El Tigre Mine, Sonora," *Mexican Mining Journal* (July): 19–20.
    1908   "Report on La Republica Mine," *El Paso Mining Journal* (June): 12.

Rogers, A. P.
    1908   "Recent Mining Developments in Chihuahua," *Engineering and Mining Journal* (October): 682.

Sparks, George F., Herman E. Bateman, and Ray Brandes, eds.
    1961   "Three Years of the Diary of Henry Fountain Ashurst, 1910–1913," *Arizona and the West* (Spring): 7–38.

Sweeney, Joseph U.
    1927   "Judge Sweeney Watches A Revolution," *Password* (Summer): 68–73.

Tays, A. H.
    1907   "Present Labor Conditions in Mexico," *Engineering and Mining Journal* (October 5): 622–23.

Treadwell, John C.
   1905   "The Sahuayucan Mining District, Mexico," *Engineering and Mining Journal* (December 30): 213–16.
Vail, Richard H.
   1914   "El Paso Smelting Works," *Engineering and Mining Journal* (September 12): 465–68, and (September 19): 515–18.
Young, Otis E.
   1965   "The Spanish Tradition in Gold and Silver Mining," *Arizona and the West* (Winter): 302–8.

UNPUBLISHED

de Wetter, Mardee
   1946   Revolutionary El Paso, 1910–1917. M. A. thesis, Texas College of Mines and Metallurgy.
El Paso County Clerk
   undated   Probate File #20,710 (Mss. in County Clerk's Office, El Paso County, Texas).
Hoard, L. Roy
   undated   Mexico Northwestern Railway Company (typescript in L. Roy Hoard Collection, Southwest Reference, El Paso Public Library).
Lee, Mary Antoine
   1950   A Historical Survey of the American Smelting and Refining Company in El Paso, 1887–1950. M. A. thesis, Texas Western College.
Mexico Northwestern Railway
   undated   Mexico Northwestern Railway Company (typescript in L. Roy Hoard Collection, Southwest Reference, El Paso Public Library).
Mining File — Mexico
   undated   Mining File — Mexico, Folder 53, Southwest Reference, El Paso Public Library.
Olk, Joan B.
   undated   The Boers in the Southwest (typescript in Southwest Reference, El Paso Public Library).
St. Clement Episcopal Church (El Paso)
   undated   Register.

Sandels, Robert Lynn
    1967   Silvestre Terrazas, the Press, and the Origins of the Mexican Revolution in Chihuahua. Ph.D. dissertation, University of Oregon.

"Sierra Madre . . ."
    undated   "Sierra Madre Railway District" (unidentified clipping in Mining File, Folder 606–40, Southwest Reference, El Paso Public Library).

Slack, J. B.
    undated   Record of Deaths at White Oaks and Vicinity from 5–15–80 to 7–3–1905 (Ms. in possession of Bill Ward, Lincoln, New Mexico).

Sutton, D. C.
    1908   Report on Cuatro Amigos Mines, District of Galeana, Chihuahua, Mexico, October 10 (typescript in Mining File, Folder 606–40, Southwest Reference, El Paso Public Library).

Weed and Probert
    1910   Report on the Candelaria Mining Property, San Pedro, Chihuahua, Mexico, by Weed and Probert, Geological and Mining Engineers, New York and Los Angeles, July 8 (typescript in Mining Folder 606–40, Southwest Reference, El Paso Public Library).

Index